ALWAYS POSTPONE MEETINGS WITH TIME-WASTING MORONS

A DILBERT® BOOK

SCOTT ADAMS

LET ME GET BACK TO YOU ON THAT.

BOXTREE

For Pam, my role model

First published in the UK 1995 by Boxtree Limited, Broadwall House, 21 Broadwall, London SE1 9PL

First published in the USA in 1994 by Andrews and McMeel, 4900 Main Street, Kansas City, Missouri 64112, USA

Copyright © 1994 by United Feature Syndicate, Inc.

10 9 8 7 6 5 4 3 2 1

ISBN: 0 7522 0854 3

Printed and bound in Finland by WSOY

A CIP catalogue record for this book is available from the British Library

INTRODUCTION

Thank you for buying this book. My editor asked me to write an introduction and here it is. I don't have anything to say, but frankly, I doubt anybody will read the introduction anyway; unless you're on a long plane ride and you've already read everything else including the barf bag instructions, and you're looking desperately for something you haven't read—something to take your mind off the fact that most commercial aircraft fleets are well beyond their intended technological life, and the chances are very good that you will soon be engulfed in flames, racing toward the ground at Mach One while cursing yourself for not listening to the pre-flight safety instructions. No, you had to be nonchalant and conspicuously ignore the flight attendant, like you're some kind of big-time traveller or something. And now, because of your ego, they'll be sifting the wreckage for enough of your bony matter to fill an envelope with your name on it. And the guy sitting next to you will be interviewed on CNN saying how he watched you being devoured by flames from the comfort of his emergency asbestos suit which he knew how to get into because **he** paid attention to the flight attendant. But I digress.

The point is that I have to write this introduction. I'm almost done. I think it's going pretty well so far. Okay, I'm done.

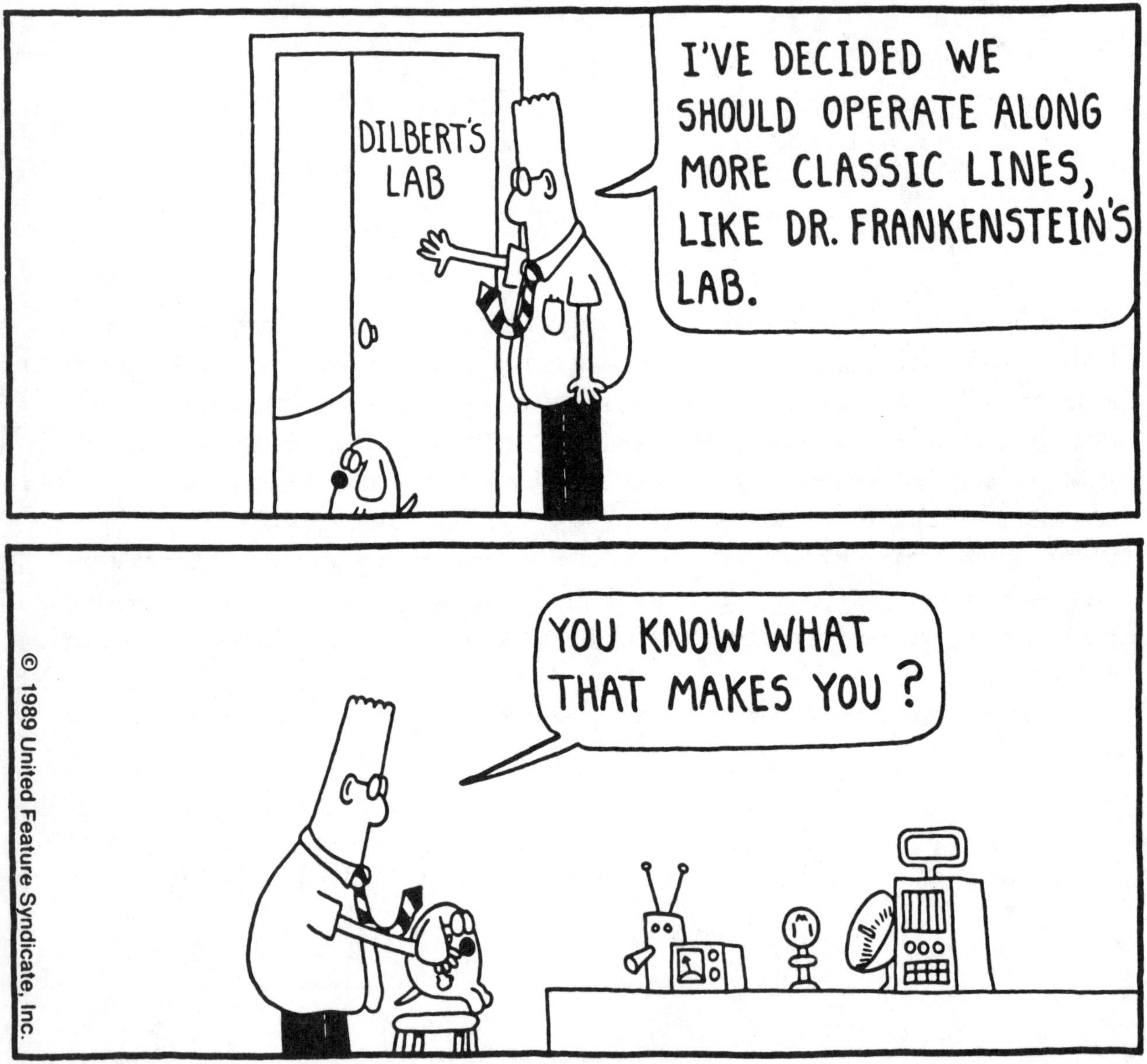
DILBERT'S LAB
I'VE DECIDED WE SHOULD OPERATE ALONG MORE CLASSIC LINES, LIKE DR. FRANKENSTEIN'S LAB.
YOU KNOW WHAT THAT MAKES YOU ?

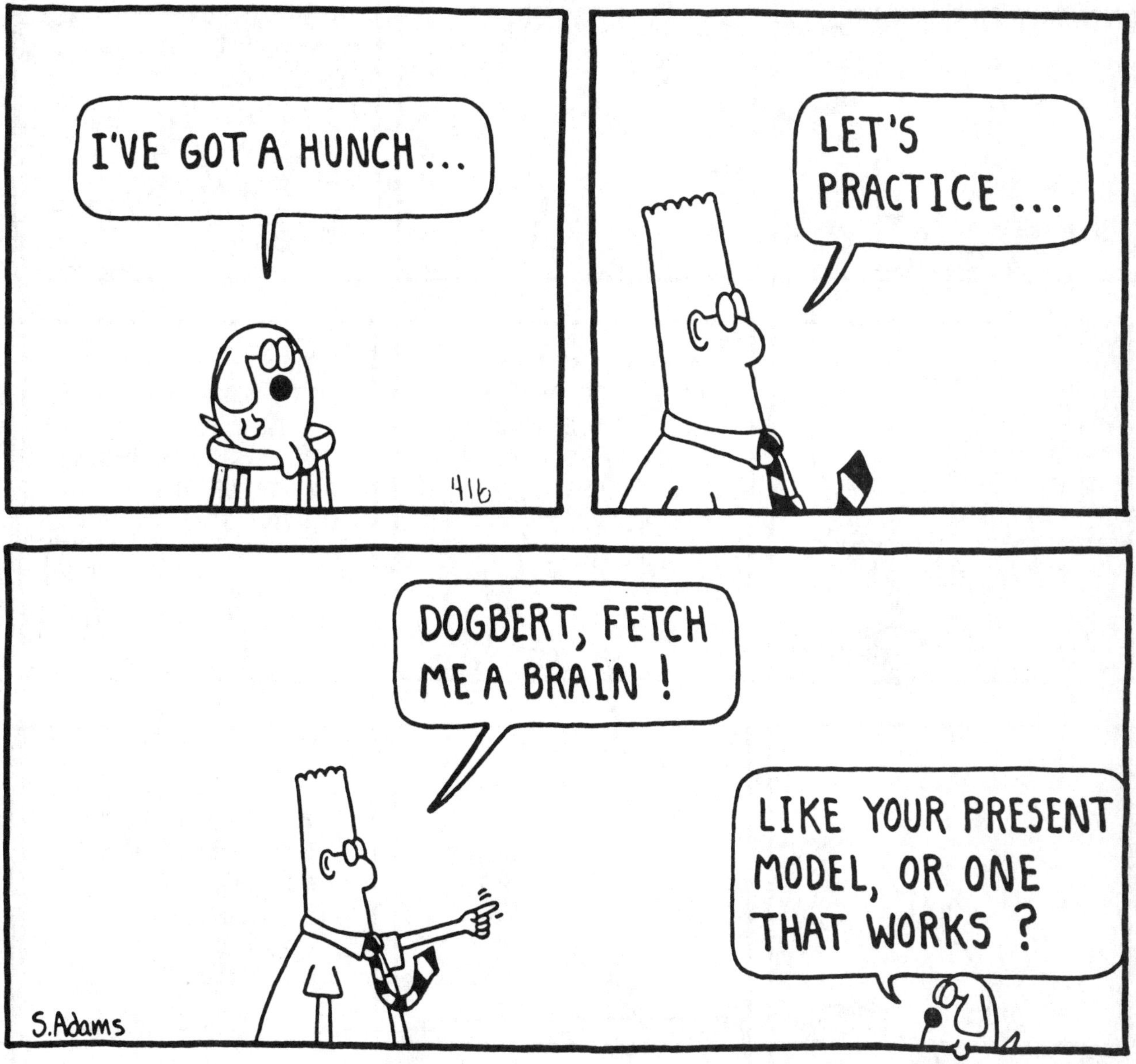
I'VE GOT A HUNCH...
416
LET'S PRACTICE...
DOGBERT, FETCH ME A BRAIN!
LIKE YOUR PRESENT MODEL, OR ONE THAT WORKS?
S.Adams

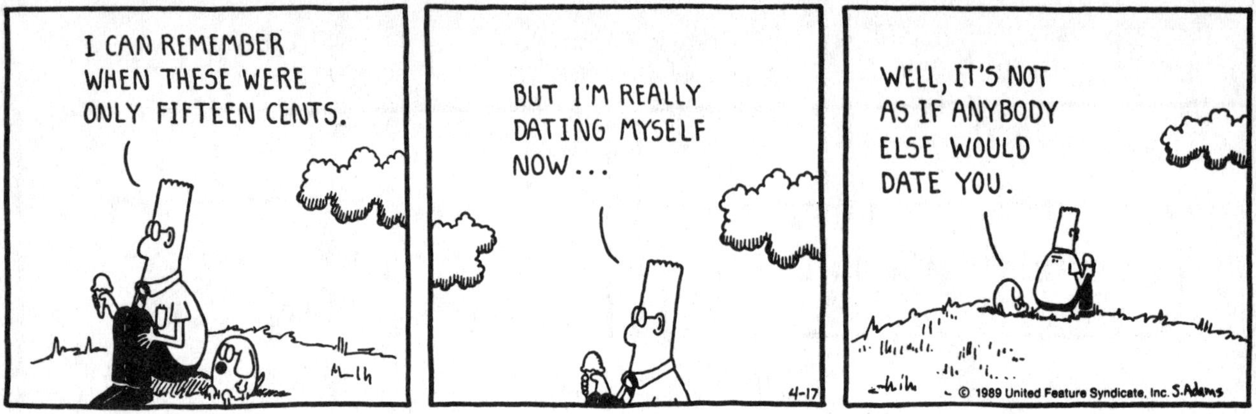
I CAN REMEMBER WHEN THESE WERE ONLY FIFTEEN CENTS.
BUT I'M REALLY DATING MYSELF NOW...
4-17
WELL, IT'S NOT AS IF ANYBODY ELSE WOULD DATE YOU.
© 1989 United Feature Syndicate, Inc. S.Adams

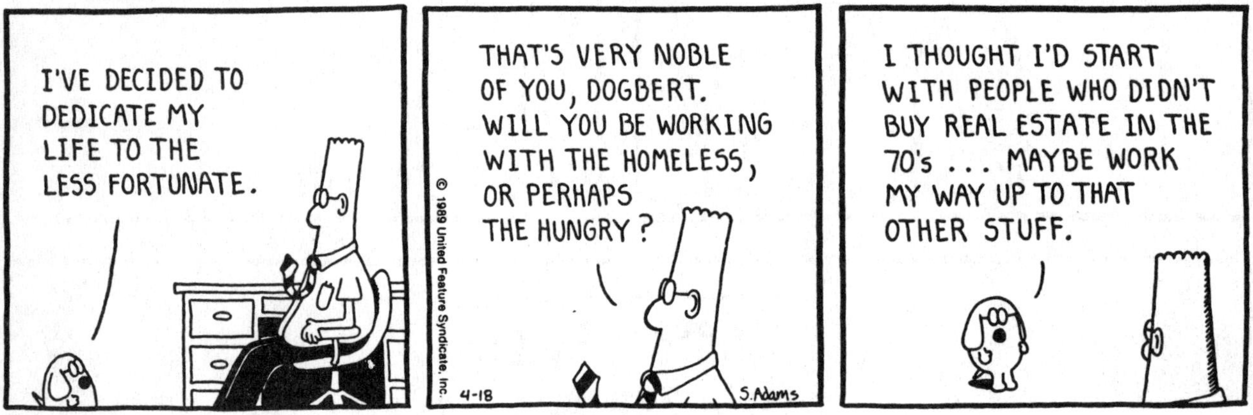
I'VE DECIDED TO DEDICATE MY LIFE TO THE LESS FORTUNATE.
© 1989 United Feature Syndicate, Inc.
4-18
THAT'S VERY NOBLE OF YOU, DOGBERT. WILL YOU BE WORKING WITH THE HOMELESS, OR PERHAPS THE HUNGRY?
S.Adams
I THOUGHT I'D START WITH PEOPLE WHO DIDN'T BUY REAL ESTATE IN THE 70's ... MAYBE WORK MY WAY UP TO THAT OTHER STUFF.

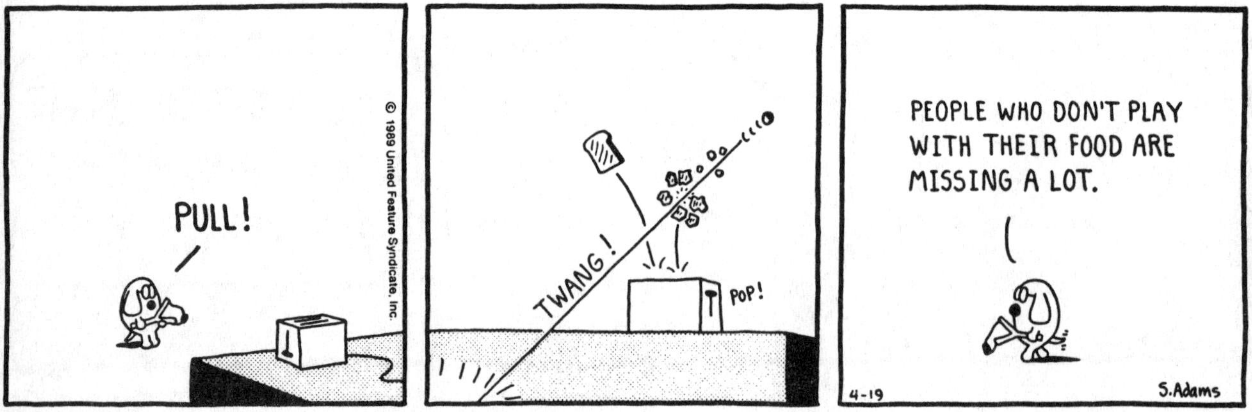
PULL!
© 1989 United Feature Syndicate, Inc.
TWANG!
POP!
PEOPLE WHO DON'T PLAY WITH THEIR FOOD ARE MISSING A LOT.
4-19
S.Adams

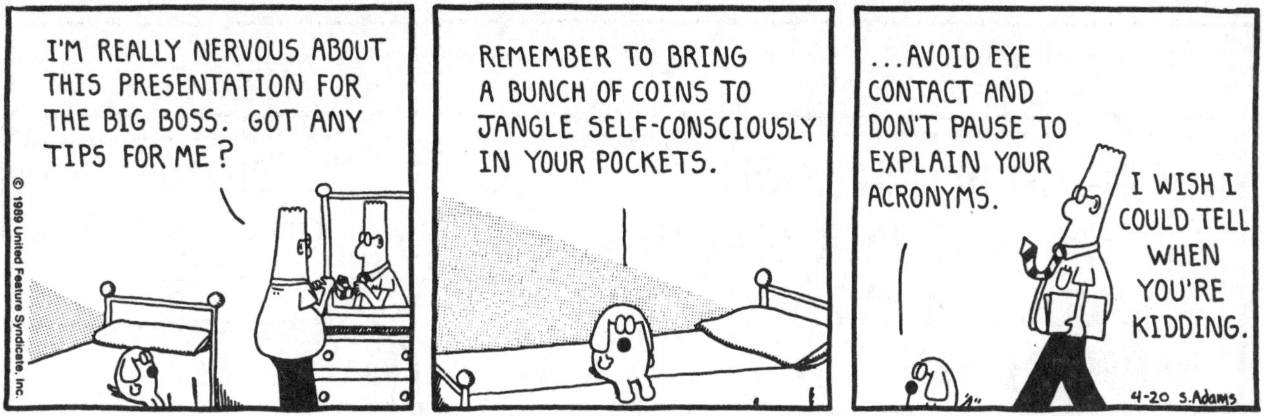
I'M REALLY NERVOUS ABOUT THIS PRESENTATION FOR THE BIG BOSS. GOT ANY TIPS FOR ME?
© 1989 United Feature Syndicate, Inc.
REMEMBER TO BRING A BUNCH OF COINS TO JANGLE SELF-CONSCIOUSLY IN YOUR POCKETS.
...AVOID EYE CONTACT AND DON'T PAUSE TO EXPLAIN YOUR ACRONYMS.
I WISH I COULD TELL WHEN YOU'RE KIDDING.
4-20 S.Adams

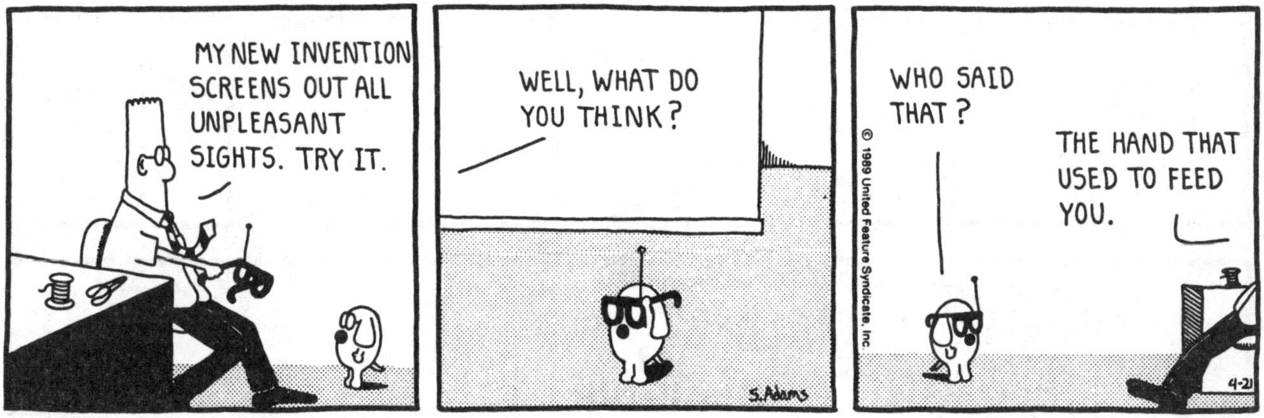
MY NEW INVENTION SCREENS OUT ALL UNPLEASANT SIGHTS. TRY IT.
WELL, WHAT DO YOU THINK?
S.Adams
WHO SAID THAT?
THE HAND THAT USED TO FEED YOU.
© 1989 United Feature Syndicate, Inc.
4-21

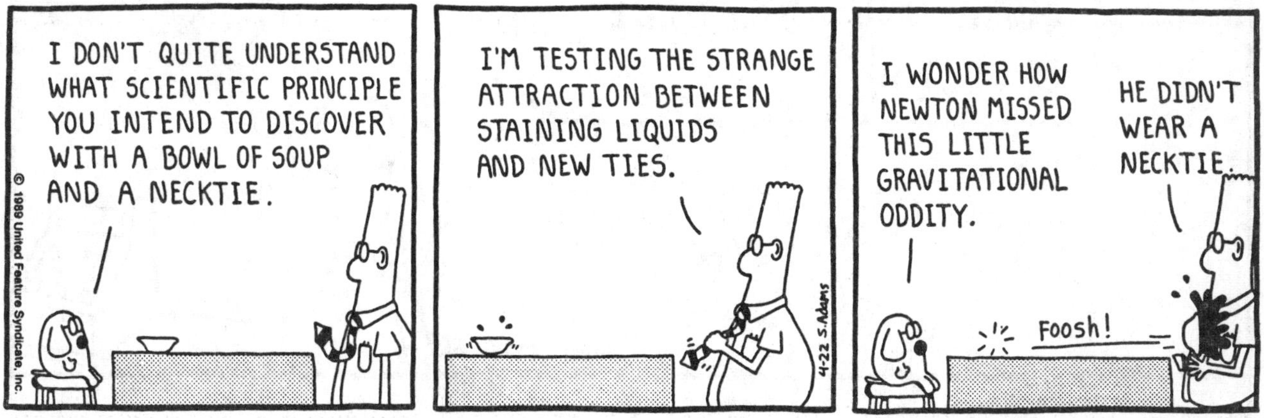
I DON'T QUITE UNDERSTAND WHAT SCIENTIFIC PRINCIPLE YOU INTEND TO DISCOVER WITH A BOWL OF SOUP AND A NECKTIE.
© 1989 United Feature Syndicate, Inc.
I'M TESTING THE STRANGE ATTRACTION BETWEEN STAINING LIQUIDS AND NEW TIES.
4-22 S.Adams
I WONDER HOW NEWTON MISSED THIS LITTLE GRAVITATIONAL ODDITY.
Foosh!
HE DIDN'T WEAR A NECKTIE.

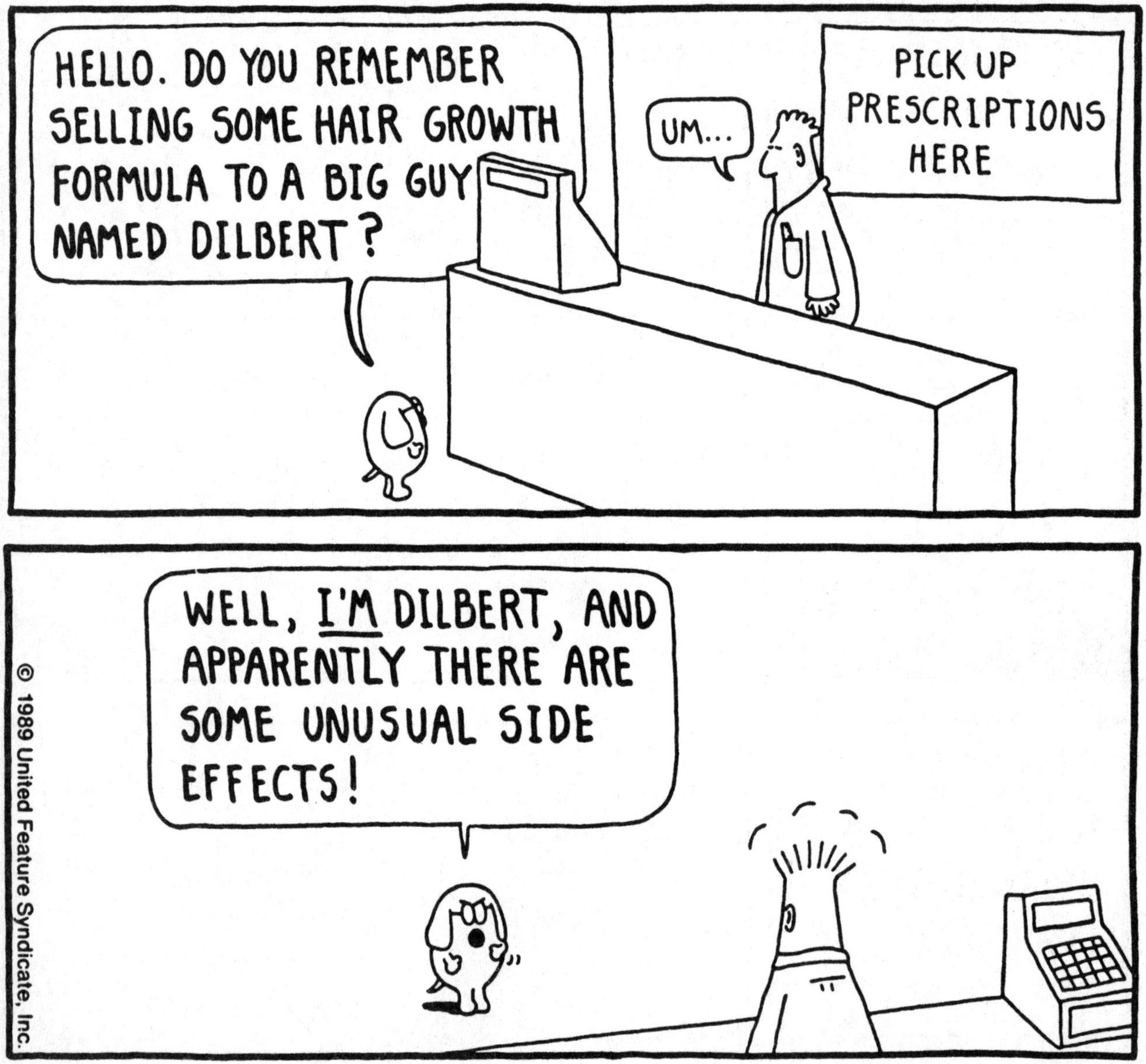
HELLO. DO YOU REMEMBER SELLING SOME HAIR GROWTH FORMULA TO A BIG GUY NAMED DILBERT?
UM...
PICK UP PRESCRIPTIONS HERE
WELL, I'M DILBERT, AND APPARENTLY THERE ARE SOME UNUSUAL SIDE EFFECTS!

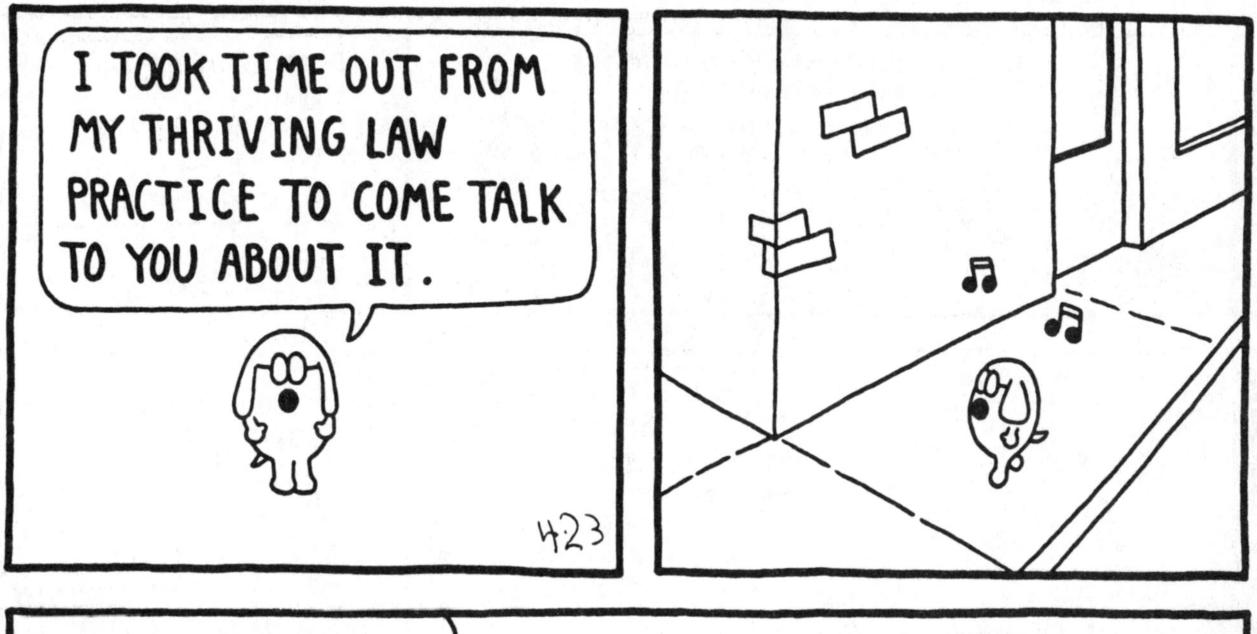
I TOOK TIME OUT FROM MY THRIVING LAW PRACTICE TO COME TALK TO YOU ABOUT IT.
4-23
THANKS DOGBERT, BUT I ONLY ASKED YOU TO GET MY PRESCRIPTION REFILL ... NOT THE DEED TO THE PHARMACY.
IN THE LONG RUN THIS IS MORE COST-EFFECTIVE.
S. Adams

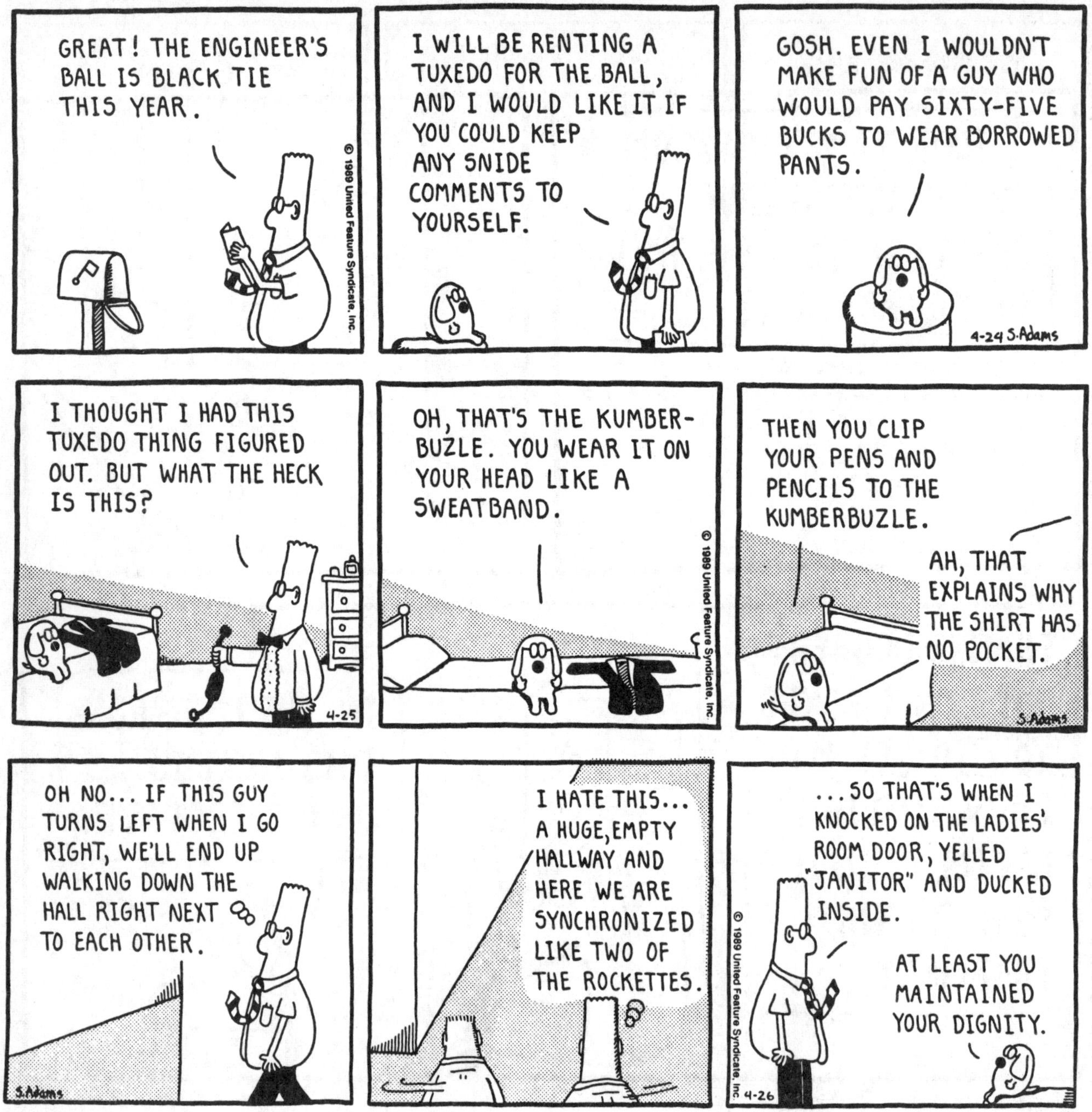
GREAT! THE ENGINEER'S BALL IS BLACK TIE THIS YEAR.
© 1989 United Feature Syndicate, Inc.
I WILL BE RENTING A TUXEDO FOR THE BALL, AND I WOULD LIKE IT IF YOU COULD KEEP ANY SNIDE COMMENTS TO YOURSELF.
GOSH. EVEN I WOULDN'T MAKE FUN OF A GUY WHO WOULD PAY SIXTY-FIVE BUCKS TO WEAR BORROWED PANTS.
4-24 S. Adams
I THOUGHT I HAD THIS TUXEDO THING FIGURED OUT. BUT WHAT THE HECK IS THIS?
4-25
OH, THAT'S THE KUMBER-BUZLE. YOU WEAR IT ON YOUR HEAD LIKE A SWEATBAND.
© 1989 United Feature Syndicate, Inc.
THEN YOU CLIP YOUR PENS AND PENCILS TO THE KUMBERBUZLE.
AH, THAT EXPLAINS WHY THE SHIRT HAS NO POCKET.
S. Adams
OH NO... IF THIS GUY TURNS LEFT WHEN I GO RIGHT, WE'LL END UP WALKING DOWN THE HALL RIGHT NEXT TO EACH OTHER.
S. Adams
I HATE THIS... A HUGE, EMPTY HALLWAY AND HERE WE ARE SYNCHRONIZED LIKE TWO OF THE ROCKETTES.
© 1989 United Feature Syndicate, Inc.
...SO THAT'S WHEN I KNOCKED ON THE LADIES' ROOM DOOR, YELLED "JANITOR" AND DUCKED INSIDE.
AT LEAST YOU MAINTAINED YOUR DIGNITY.
4-26

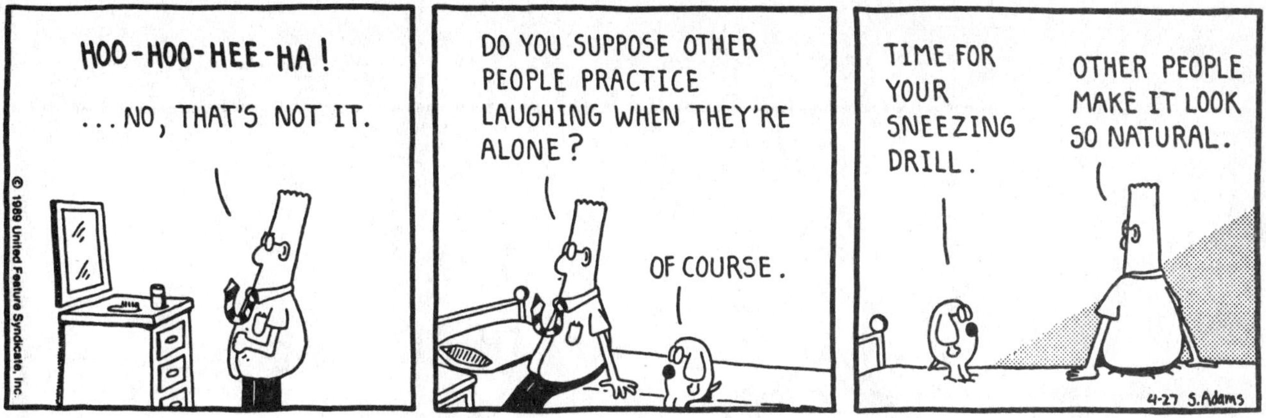
HOO-HOO-HEE-HA!
...NO, THAT'S NOT IT.
© 1989 United Feature Syndicate, Inc.
DO YOU SUPPOSE OTHER PEOPLE PRACTICE LAUGHING WHEN THEY'RE ALONE?
OF COURSE.
TIME FOR YOUR SNEEZING DRILL.
OTHER PEOPLE MAKE IT LOOK SO NATURAL.
4-27 S.Adams

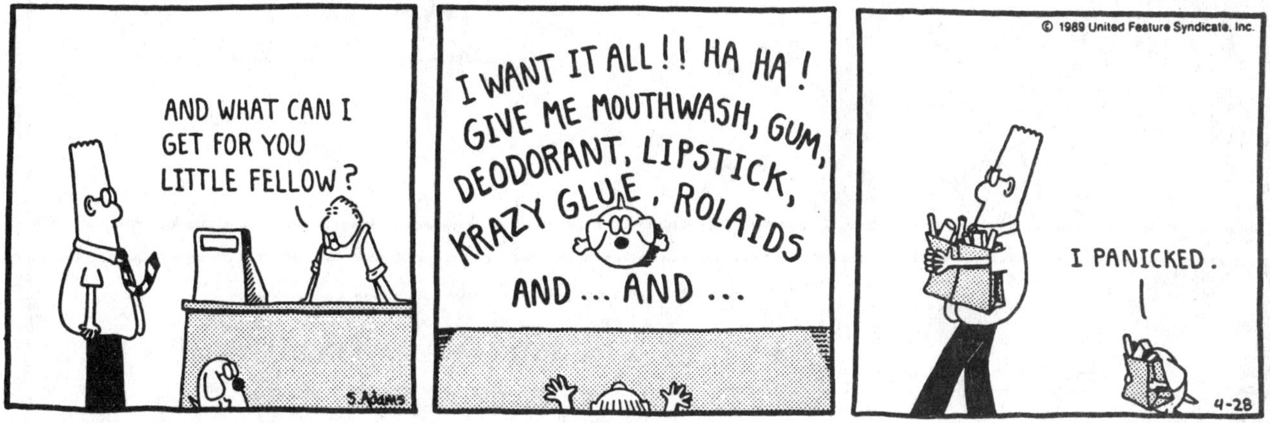
AND WHAT CAN I GET FOR YOU LITTLE FELLOW?
S.Adams
I WANT IT ALL!! HA HA!
GIVE ME MOUTHWASH, GUM, DEODORANT, LIPSTICK, KRAZY GLUE, ROLAIDS
AND... AND...
© 1989 United Feature Syndicate, Inc.
I PANICKED.
4-28

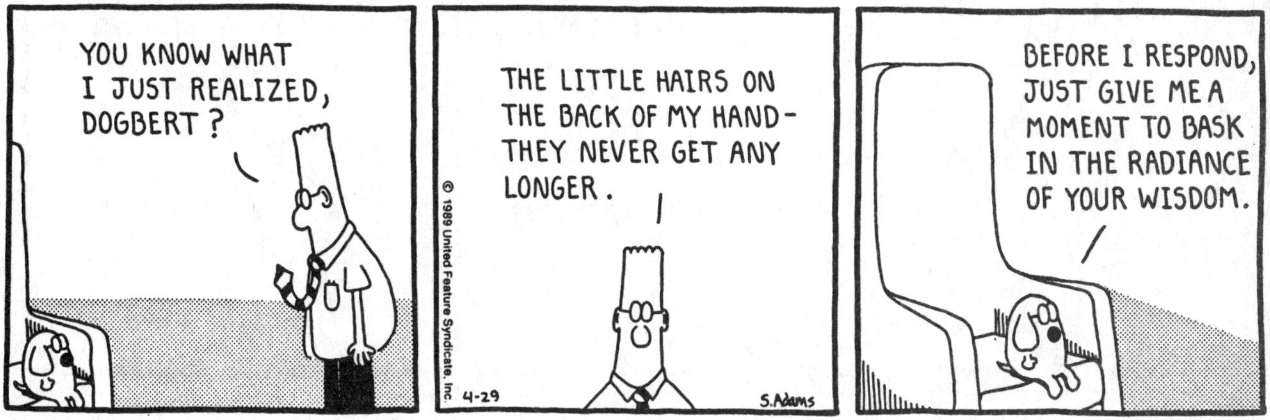
YOU KNOW WHAT I JUST REALIZED, DOGBERT?
THE LITTLE HAIRS ON THE BACK OF MY HAND- THEY NEVER GET ANY LONGER.
© 1989 United Feature Syndicate, Inc.
4-29
S.Adams
BEFORE I RESPOND, JUST GIVE ME A MOMENT TO BASK IN THE RADIANCE OF YOUR WISDOM.

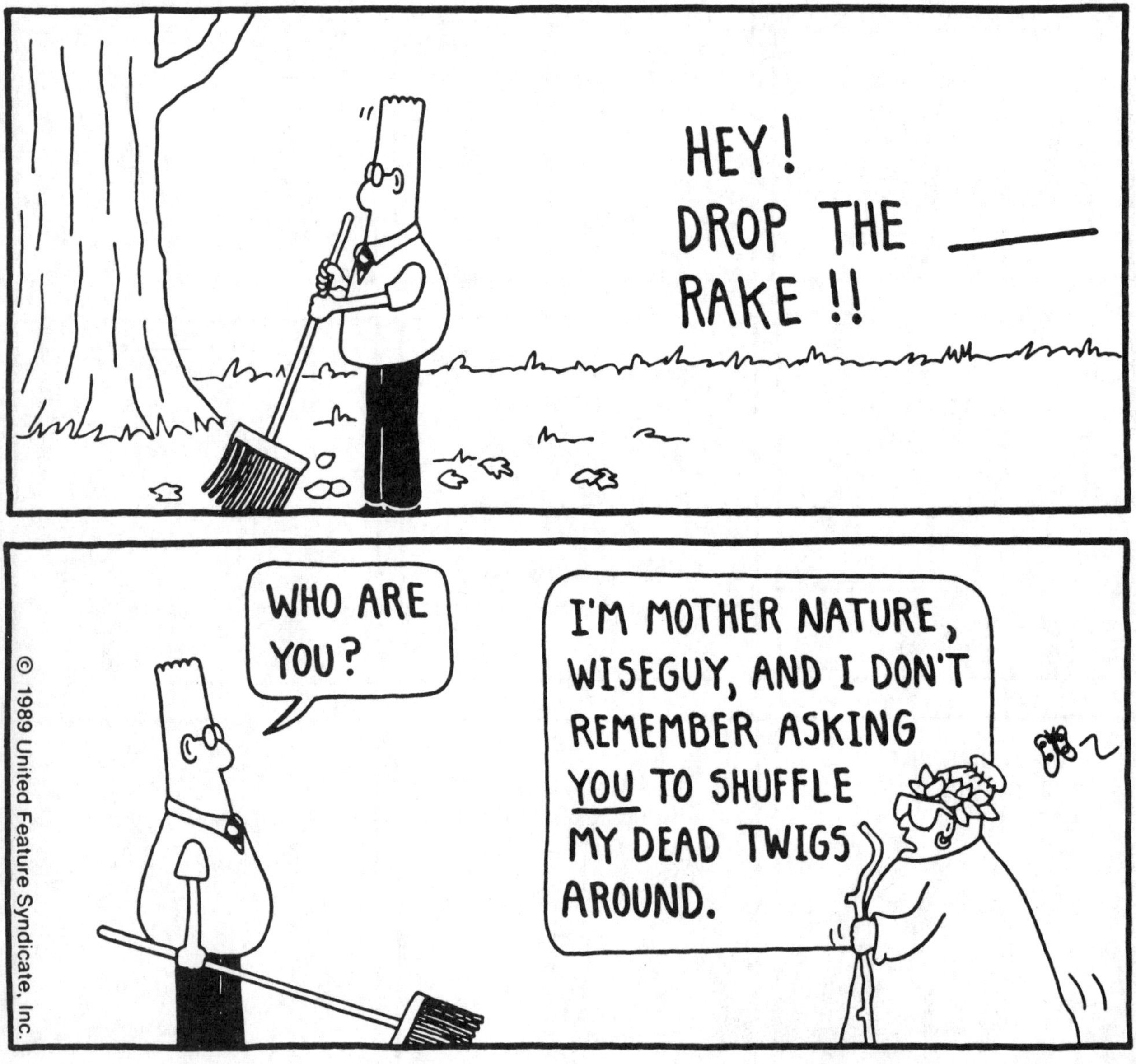
HEY! DROP THE RAKE!!
WHO ARE YOU?
I'M MOTHER NATURE, WISEGUY, AND I DON'T REMEMBER ASKING YOU TO SHUFFLE MY DEAD TWIGS AROUND.
© 1989 United Feature Syndicate, Inc.

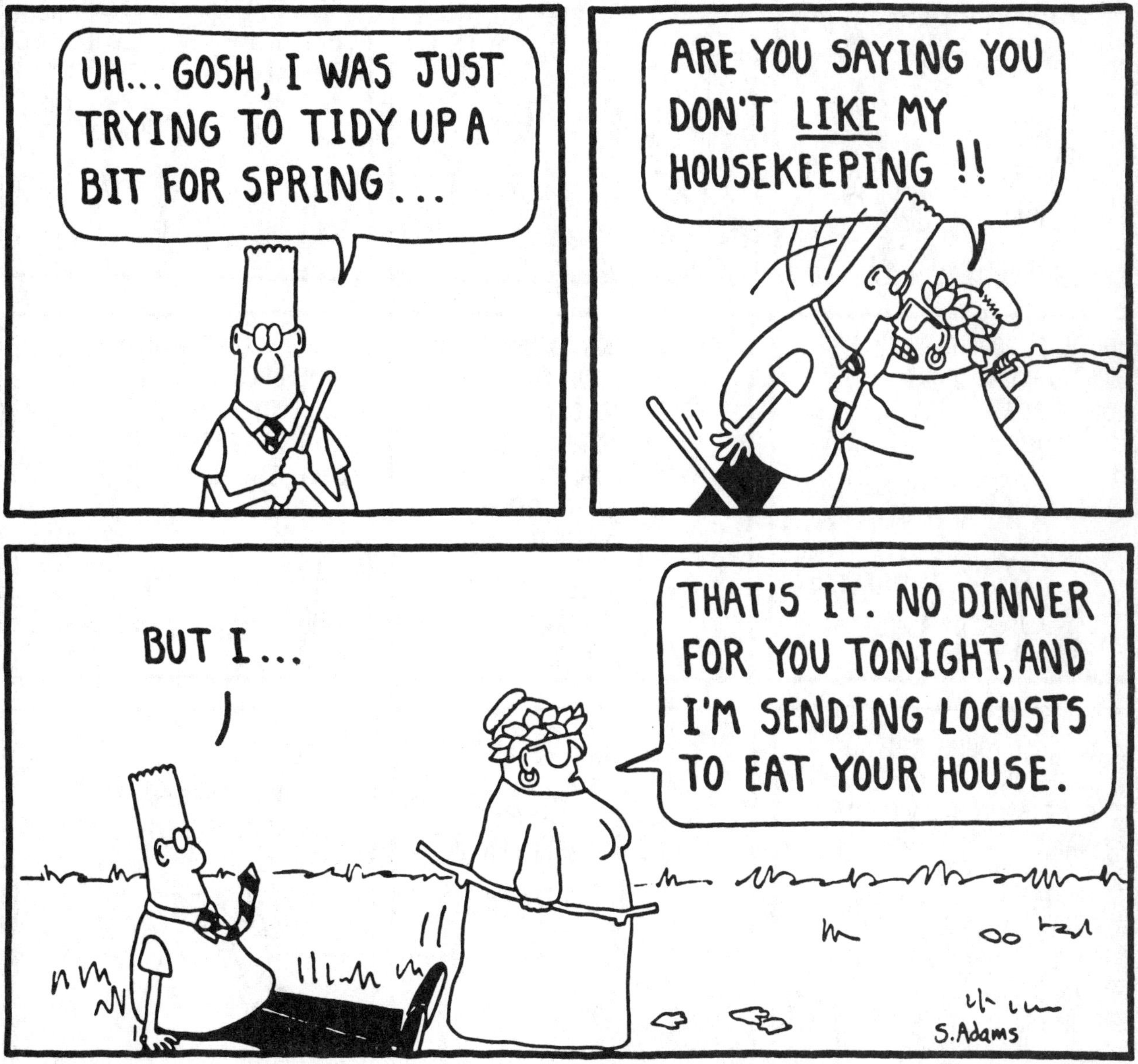
UH... GOSH, I WAS JUST TRYING TO TIDY UP A BIT FOR SPRING...
ARE YOU SAYING YOU DON'T LIKE MY HOUSEKEEPING !!
BUT I...
THAT'S IT. NO DINNER FOR YOU TONIGHT, AND I'M SENDING LOCUSTS TO EAT YOUR HOUSE.
S. Adams

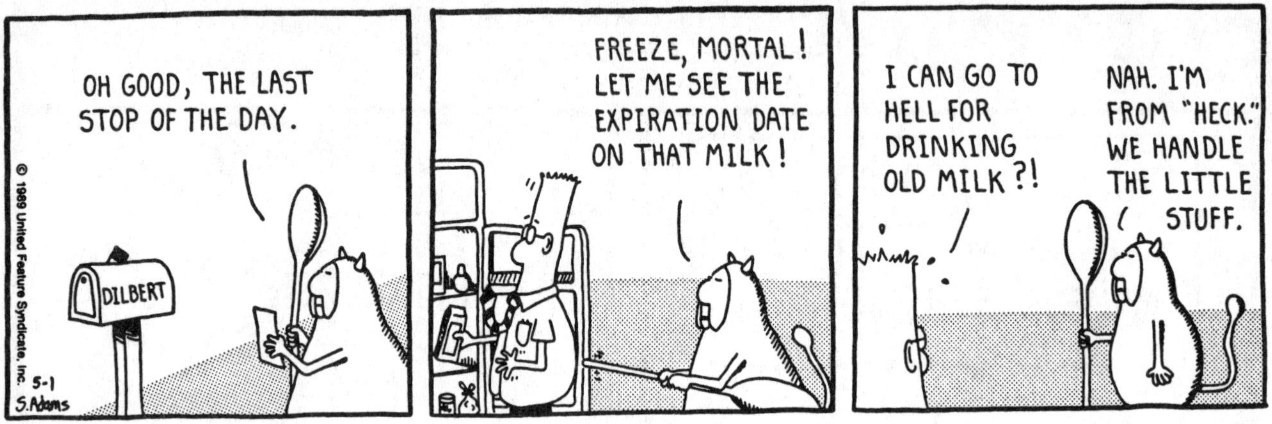
OH GOOD, THE LAST STOP OF THE DAY.
DILBERT
© 1989 United Feature Syndicate, Inc.
5-1
S.Adams
FREEZE, MORTAL! LET ME SEE THE EXPIRATION DATE ON THAT MILK!
I CAN GO TO HELL FOR DRINKING OLD MILK?!
NAH. I'M FROM "HECK." WE HANDLE THE LITTLE STUFF.

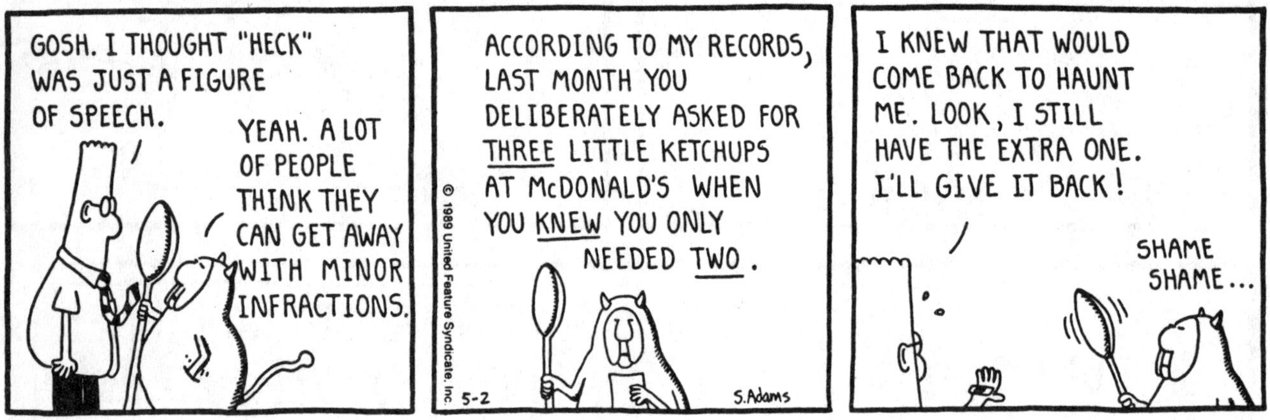
GOSH. I THOUGHT "HECK" WAS JUST A FIGURE OF SPEECH.
YEAH. A LOT OF PEOPLE THINK THEY CAN GET AWAY WITH MINOR INFRACTIONS.
© 1989 United Feature Syndicate, Inc.
ACCORDING TO MY RECORDS, LAST MONTH YOU DELIBERATELY ASKED FOR THREE LITTLE KETCHUPS AT McDONALD'S WHEN YOU KNEW YOU ONLY NEEDED TWO.
5-2
S.Adams
I KNEW THAT WOULD COME BACK TO HAUNT ME. LOOK, I STILL HAVE THE EXTRA ONE. I'LL GIVE IT BACK!
SHAME SHAME...

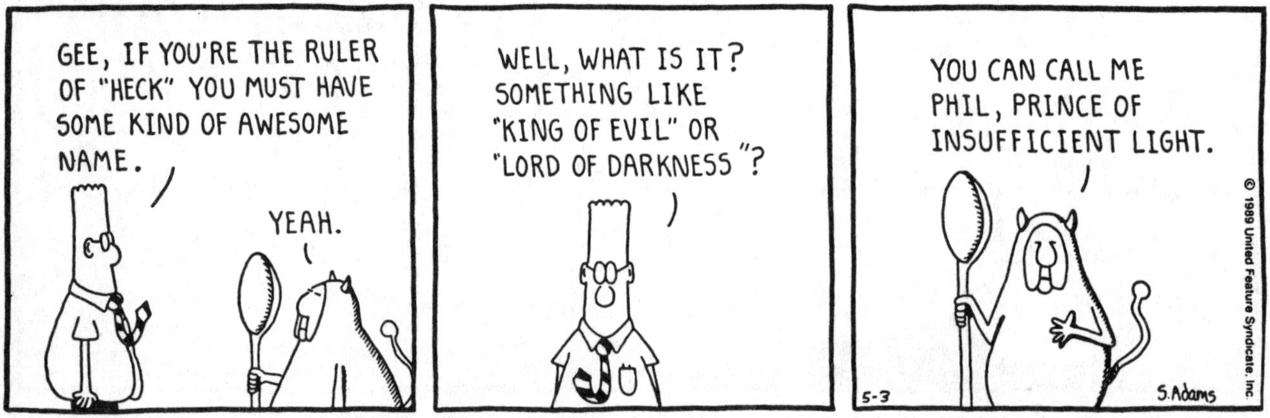
GEE, IF YOU'RE THE RULER OF "HECK" YOU MUST HAVE SOME KIND OF AWESOME NAME.
YEAH.
WELL, WHAT IS IT? SOMETHING LIKE "KING OF EVIL" OR "LORD OF DARKNESS"?
YOU CAN CALL ME PHIL, PRINCE OF INSUFFICIENT LIGHT.
© 1989 United Feature Syndicate, Inc.
5-3
S.Adams

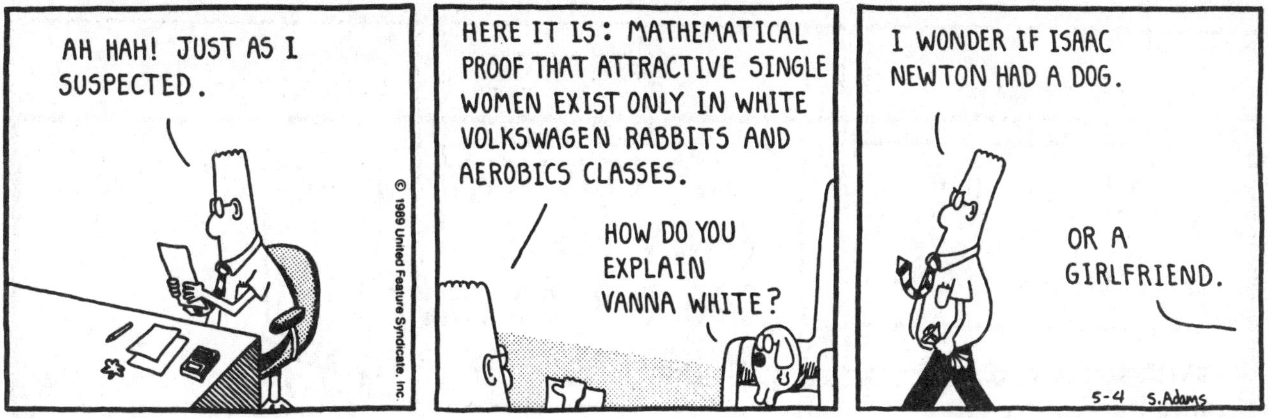
AH HAH! JUST AS I SUSPECTED.
© 1989 United Feature Syndicate, Inc.
HERE IT IS: MATHEMATICAL PROOF THAT ATTRACTIVE SINGLE WOMEN EXIST ONLY IN WHITE VOLKSWAGEN RABBITS AND AEROBICS CLASSES.
HOW DO YOU EXPLAIN VANNA WHITE?
I WONDER IF ISAAC NEWTON HAD A DOG.
OR A GIRLFRIEND.
5-4 S.Adams

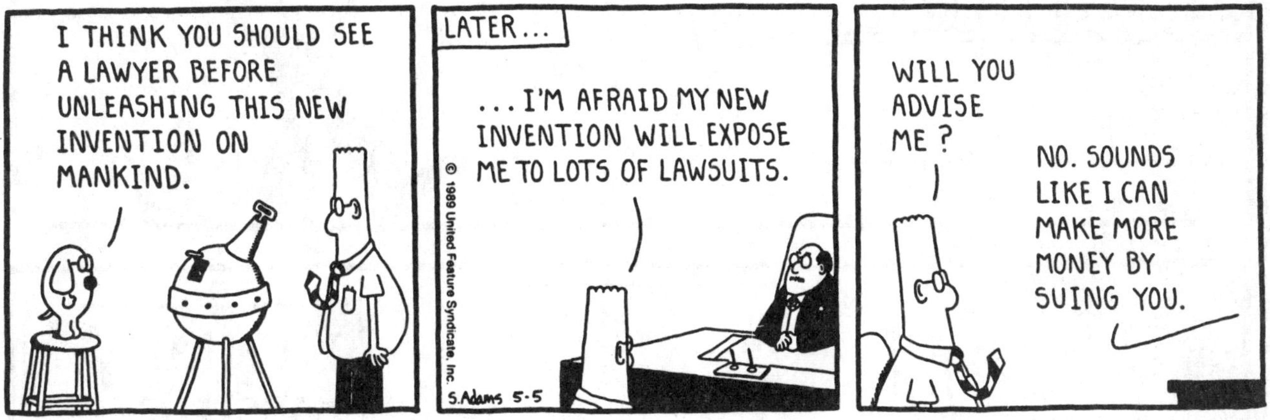
I THINK YOU SHOULD SEE A LAWYER BEFORE UNLEASHING THIS NEW INVENTION ON MANKIND.
LATER...
...I'M AFRAID MY NEW INVENTION WILL EXPOSE ME TO LOTS OF LAWSUITS.
© 1989 United Feature Syndicate, Inc.
S.Adams 5-5
WILL YOU ADVISE ME?
NO. SOUNDS LIKE I CAN MAKE MORE MONEY BY SUING YOU.

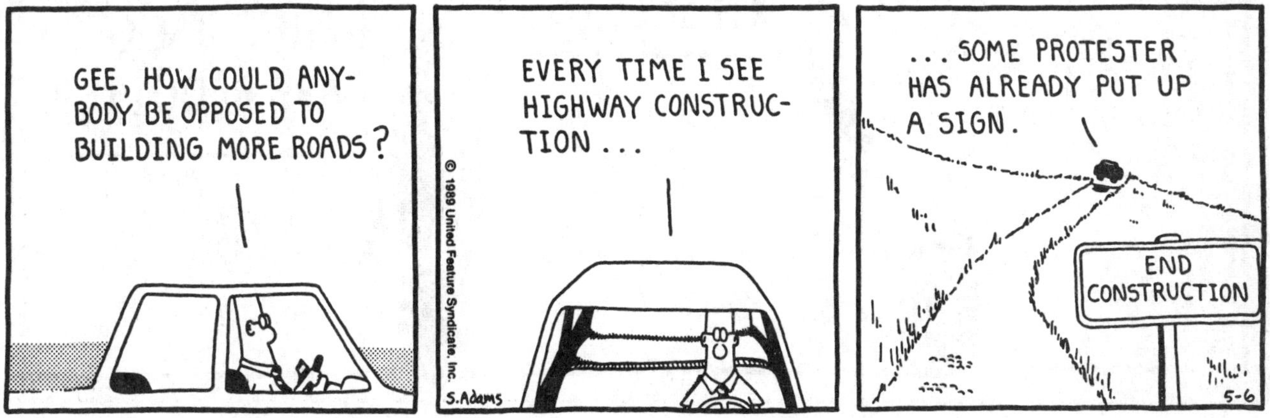
GEE, HOW COULD ANY-BODY BE OPPOSED TO BUILDING MORE ROADS?
EVERY TIME I SEE HIGHWAY CONSTRUC-TION ...
© 1989 United Feature Syndicate, Inc.
S.Adams
...SOME PROTESTER HAS ALREADY PUT UP A SIGN.
END CONSTRUCTION
5-6

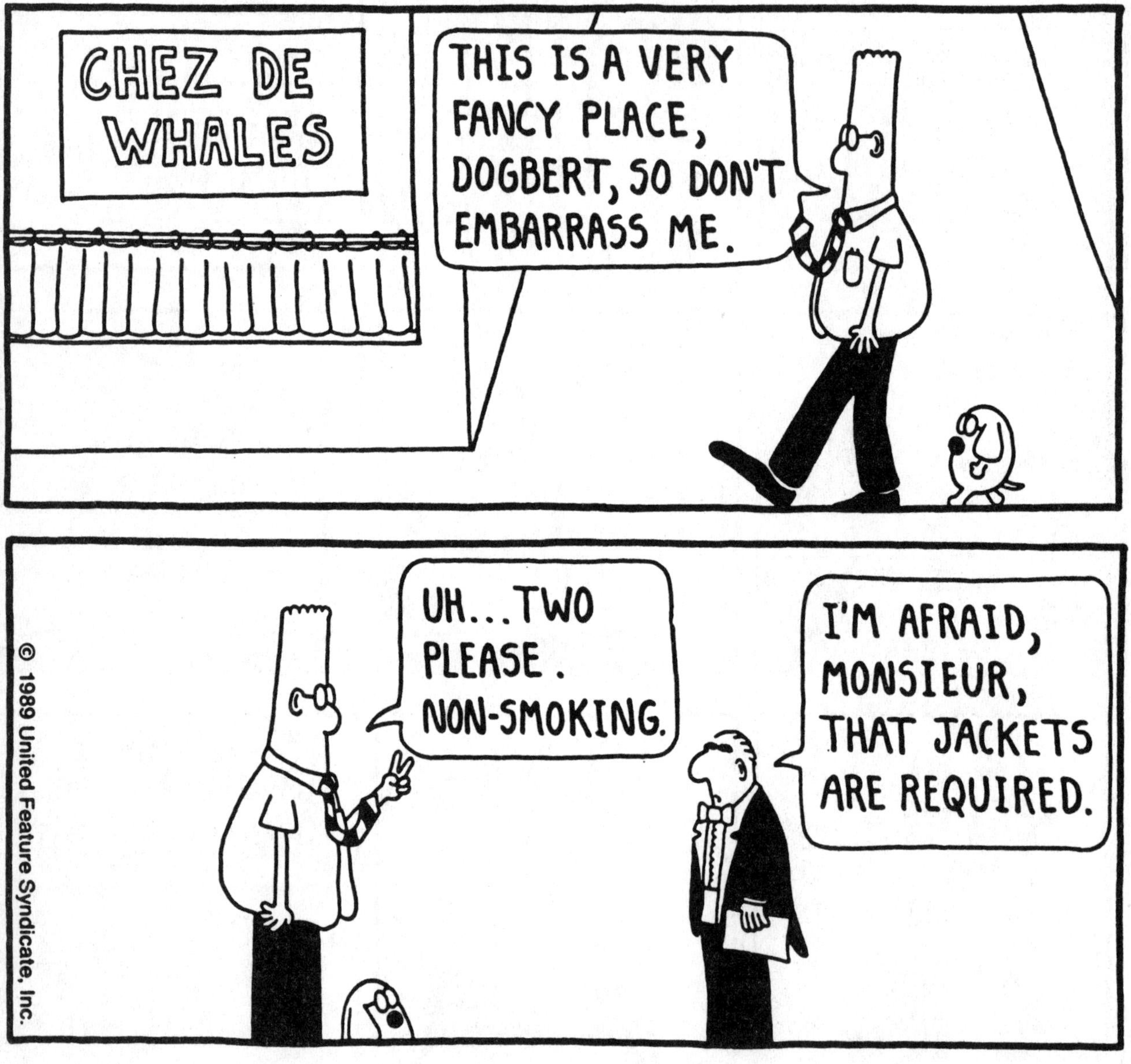
CHEZ DE WHALES
THIS IS A VERY FANCY PLACE, DOGBERT, SO DON'T EMBARRASS ME.
UH...TWO PLEASE. NON-SMOKING.
I'M AFRAID, MONSIEUR, THAT JACKETS ARE REQUIRED.
© 1989 United Feature Syndicate, Inc.

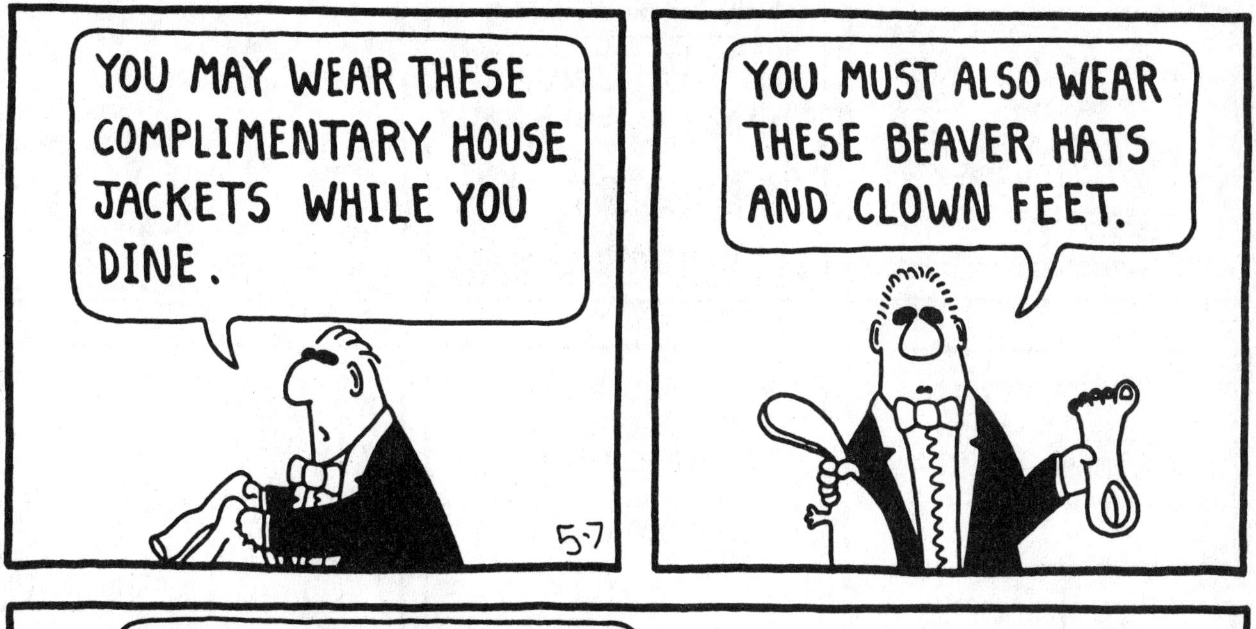
YOU MAY WEAR THESE COMPLIMENTARY HOUSE JACKETS WHILE YOU DINE.
5-7
YOU MUST ALSO WEAR THESE BEAVER HATS AND CLOWN FEET.
NEXT TIME MESSIEURS WILL REMEMBER THEIR JACKETS.
LOOKS LIKE WE NARROWLY AVOIDED EMBARRASSMENT.
S. Adams

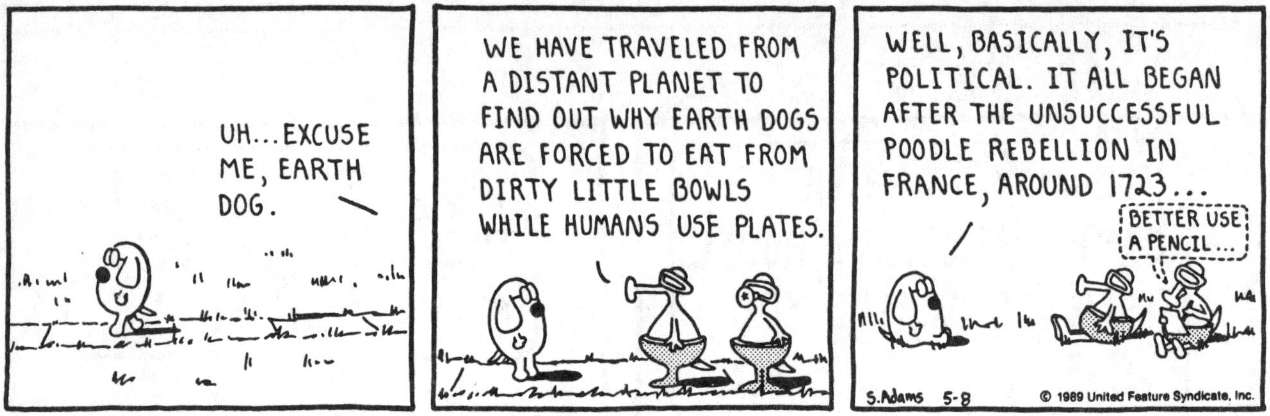
UH...EXCUSE ME, EARTH DOG.
WE HAVE TRAVELED FROM A DISTANT PLANET TO FIND OUT WHY EARTH DOGS ARE FORCED TO EAT FROM DIRTY LITTLE BOWLS WHILE HUMANS USE PLATES.
WELL, BASICALLY, IT'S POLITICAL. IT ALL BEGAN AFTER THE UNSUCCESSFUL POODLE REBELLION IN FRANCE, AROUND 1723...
BETTER USE A PENCIL...
S.Adams 5-8
© 1989 United Feature Syndicate, Inc.

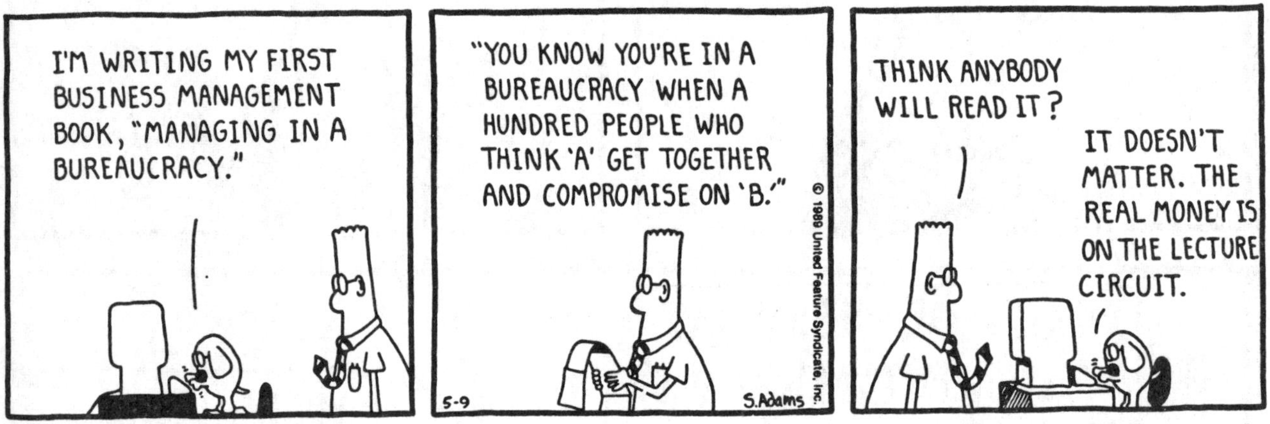
I'M WRITING MY FIRST BUSINESS MANAGEMENT BOOK, "MANAGING IN A BUREAUCRACY."
"YOU KNOW YOU'RE IN A BUREAUCRACY WHEN A HUNDRED PEOPLE WHO THINK 'A' GET TOGETHER AND COMPROMISE ON 'B.'"
5-9
S.Adams
© 1989 United Feature Syndicate, Inc.
THINK ANYBODY WILL READ IT?
IT DOESN'T MATTER. THE REAL MONEY IS ON THE LECTURE CIRCUIT.

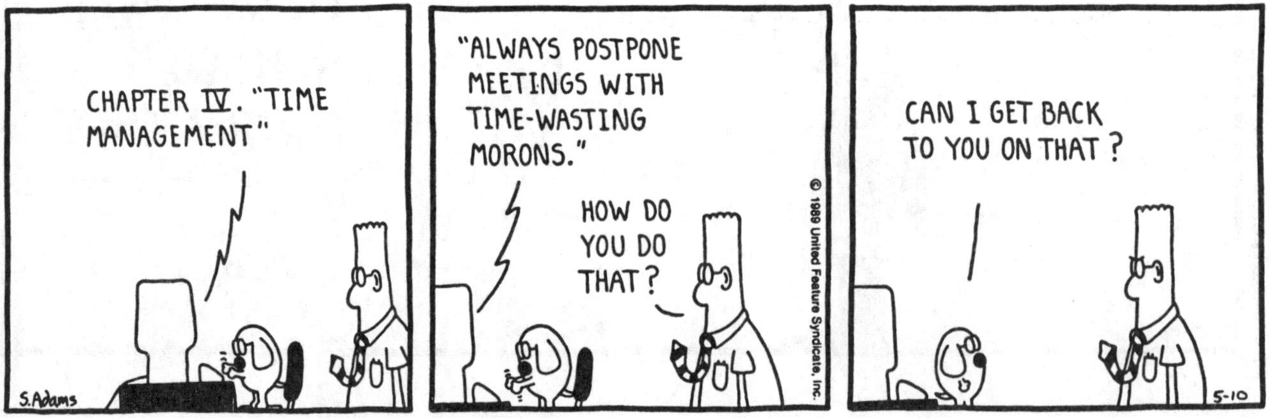
CHAPTER IV. "TIME MANAGEMENT"
S.Adams
"ALWAYS POSTPONE MEETINGS WITH TIME-WASTING MORONS."
HOW DO YOU DO THAT?
© 1989 United Feature Syndicate, Inc.
CAN I GET BACK TO YOU ON THAT?
5-10

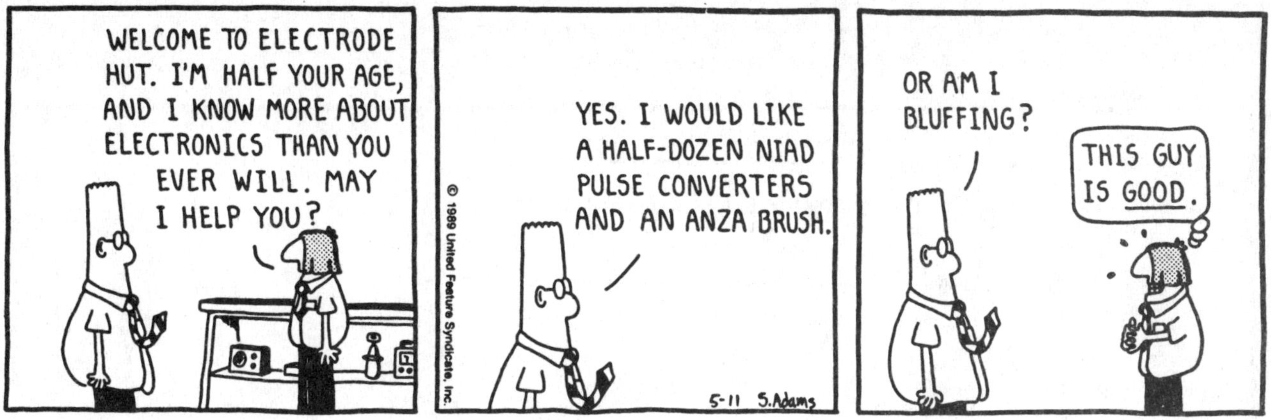
WELCOME TO ELECTRODE HUT. I'M HALF YOUR AGE, AND I KNOW MORE ABOUT ELECTRONICS THAN YOU EVER WILL. MAY I HELP YOU?
© 1989 United Feature Syndicate, Inc.
YES. I WOULD LIKE A HALF-DOZEN NIAD PULSE CONVERTERS AND AN ANZA BRUSH.
5-11 S.Adams
OR AM I BLUFFING?
THIS GUY IS GOOD.

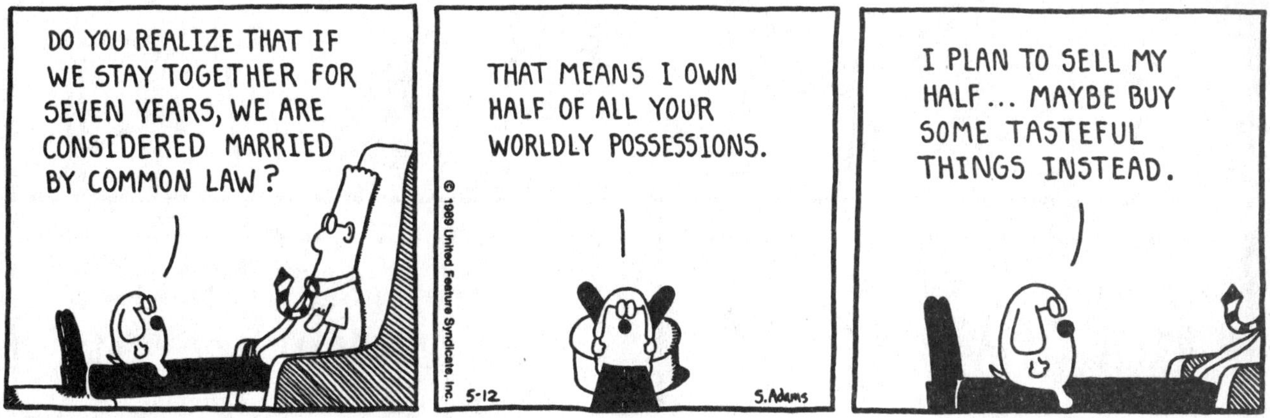
DO YOU REALIZE THAT IF WE STAY TOGETHER FOR SEVEN YEARS, WE ARE CONSIDERED MARRIED BY COMMON LAW?
© 1989 United Feature Syndicate, Inc.
THAT MEANS I OWN HALF OF ALL YOUR WORLDLY POSSESSIONS.
5-12 S.Adams
I PLAN TO SELL MY HALF... MAYBE BUY SOME TASTEFUL THINGS INSTEAD.

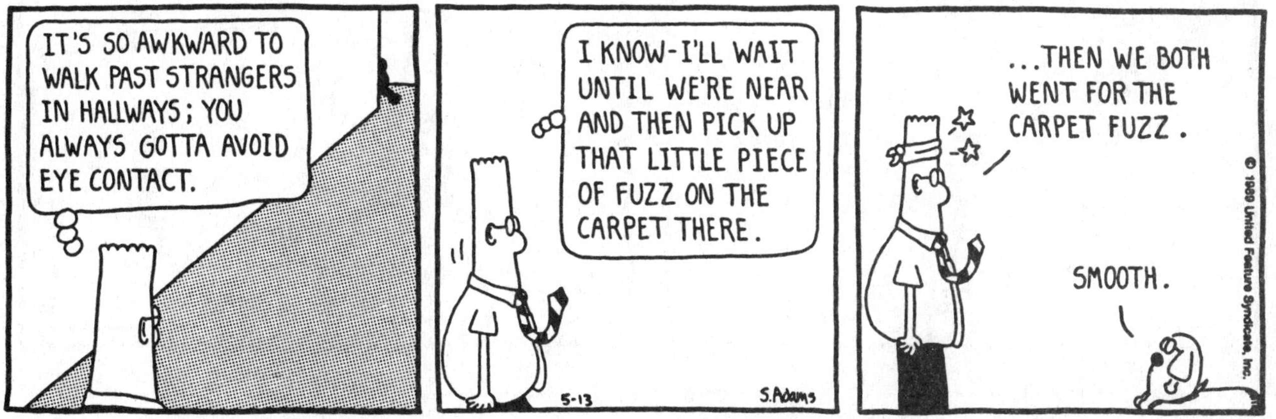
IT'S SO AWKWARD TO WALK PAST STRANGERS IN HALLWAYS; YOU ALWAYS GOTTA AVOID EYE CONTACT.
I KNOW-I'LL WAIT UNTIL WE'RE NEAR AND THEN PICK UP THAT LITTLE PIECE OF FUZZ ON THE CARPET THERE.
5-13 S.Adams
...THEN WE BOTH WENT FOR THE CARPET FUZZ.
SMOOTH.
© 1989 United Feature Syndicate, Inc.

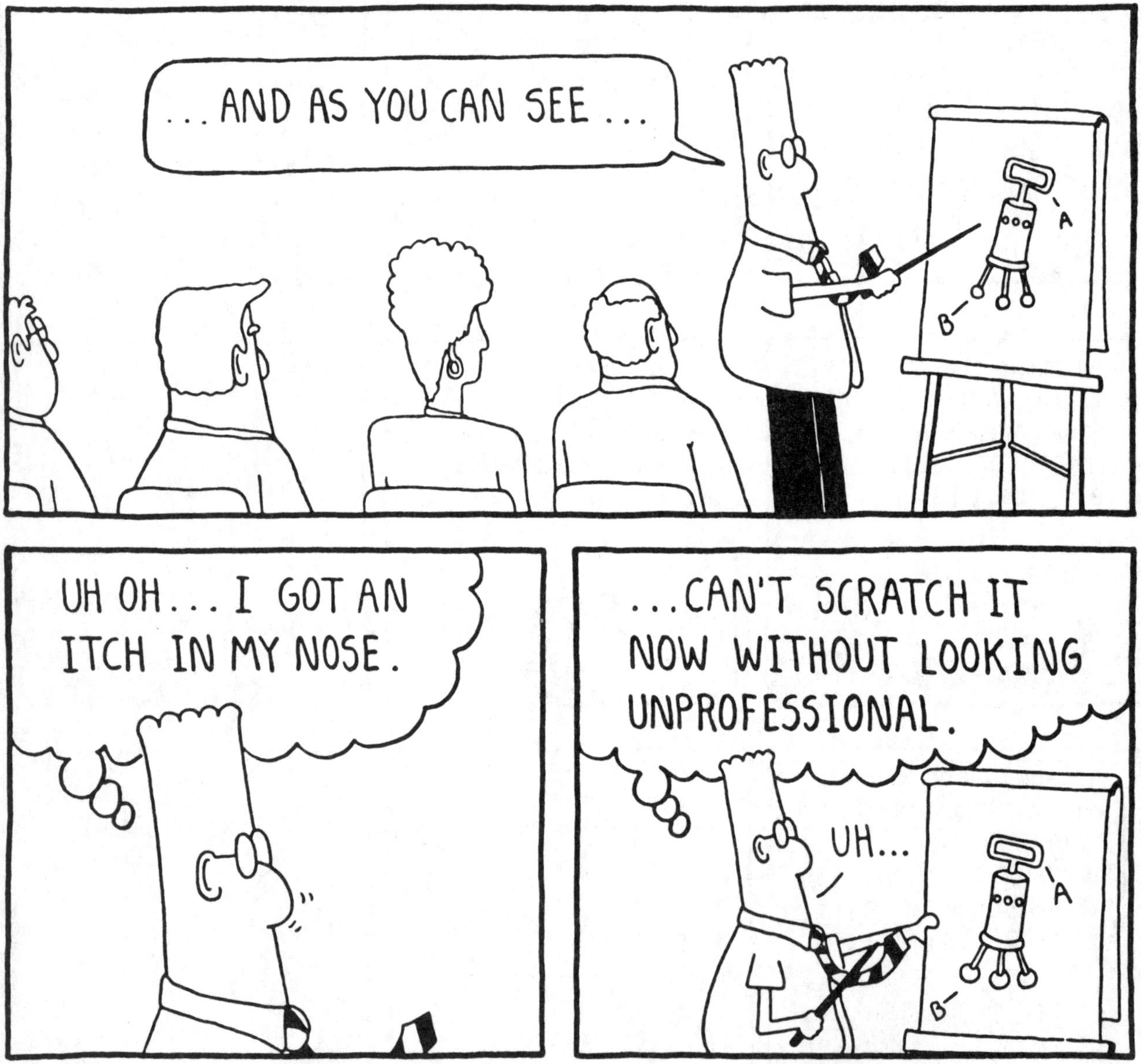
...AND AS YOU CAN SEE...
A
B
UH OH...I GOT AN ITCH IN MY NOSE.
...CAN'T SCRATCH IT NOW WITHOUT LOOKING UNPROFESSIONAL.
UH...
A
B

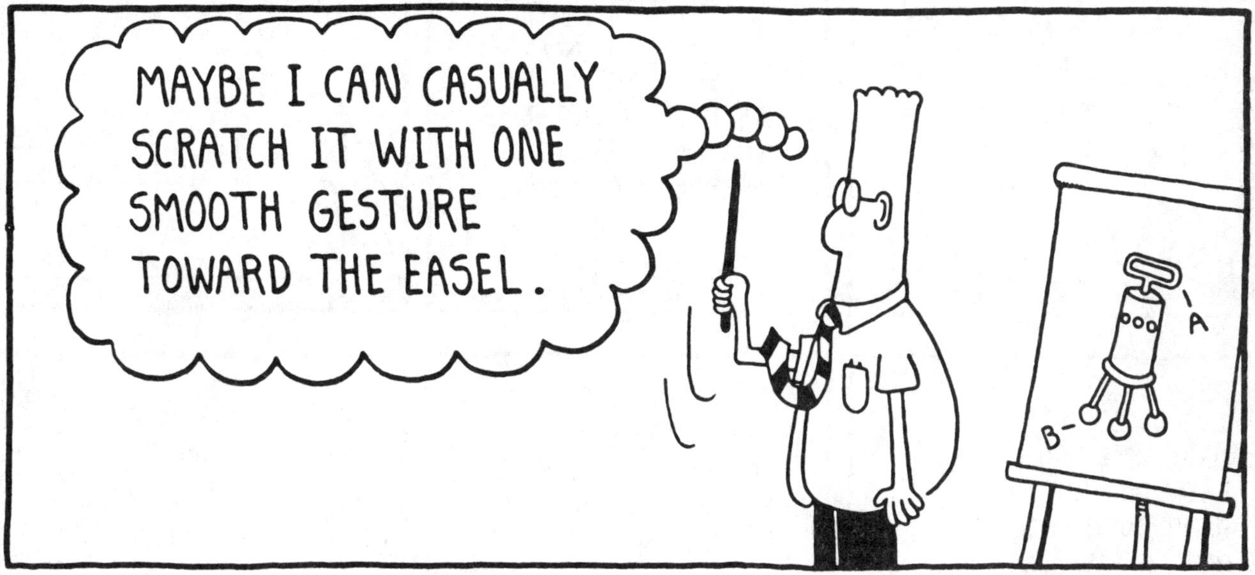
MAYBE I CAN CASUALLY SCRATCH IT WITH ONE SMOOTH GESTURE TOWARD THE EASEL.
A
B

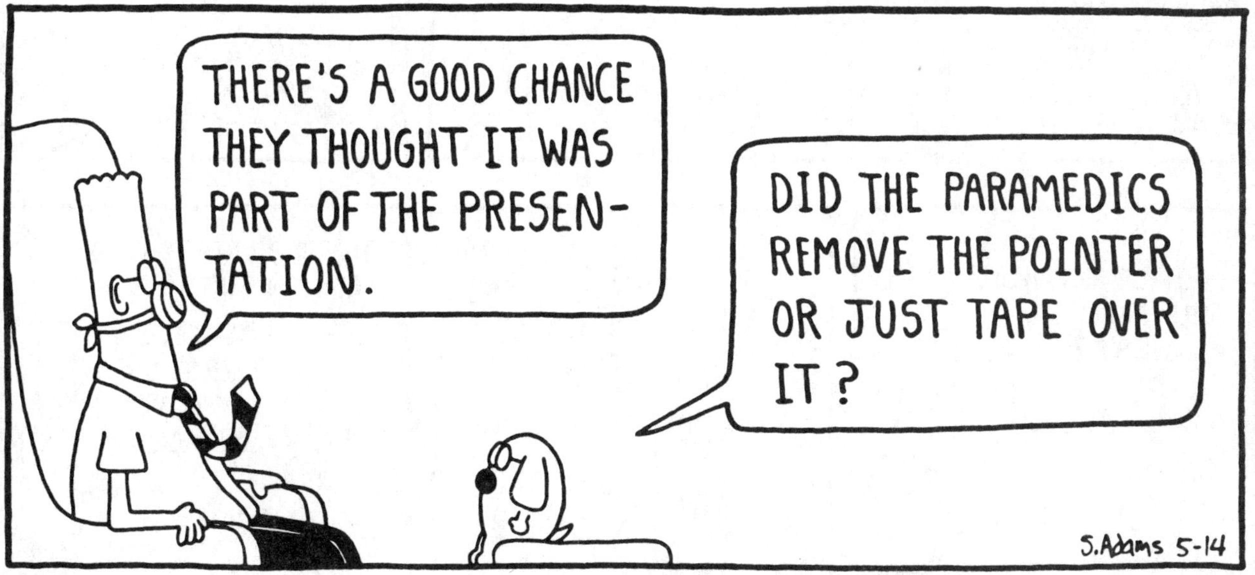
THERE'S A GOOD CHANCE THEY THOUGHT IT WAS PART OF THE PRESEN- TATION.
DID THE PARAMEDICS REMOVE THE POINTER OR JUST TAPE OVER IT?
S.Adams 5-14

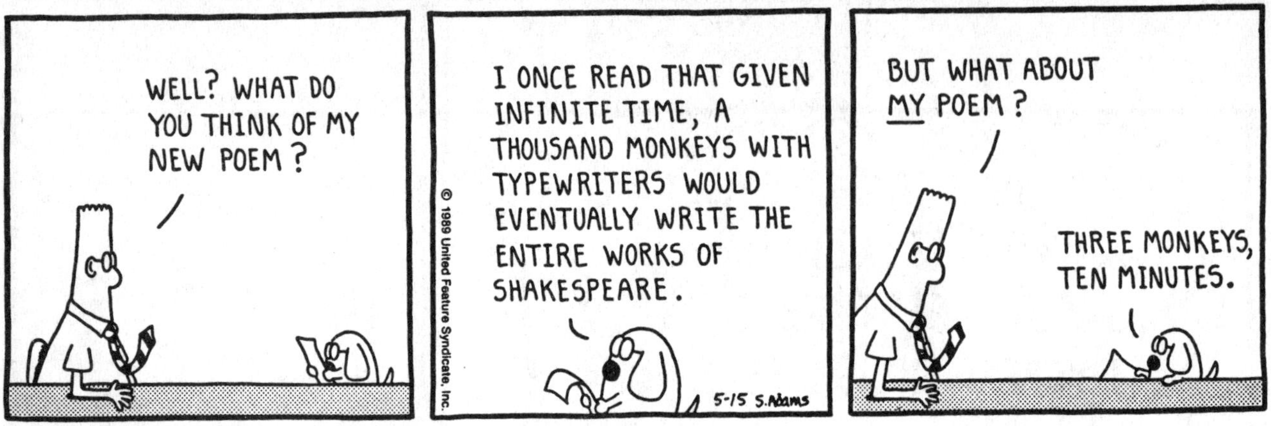
WELL? WHAT DO YOU THINK OF MY NEW POEM?
I ONCE READ THAT GIVEN INFINITE TIME, A THOUSAND MONKEYS WITH TYPEWRITERS WOULD EVENTUALLY WRITE THE ENTIRE WORKS OF SHAKESPEARE.
© 1989 United Feature Syndicate, Inc.
5-15 S.Adams
BUT WHAT ABOUT MY POEM?
THREE MONKEYS, TEN MINUTES.

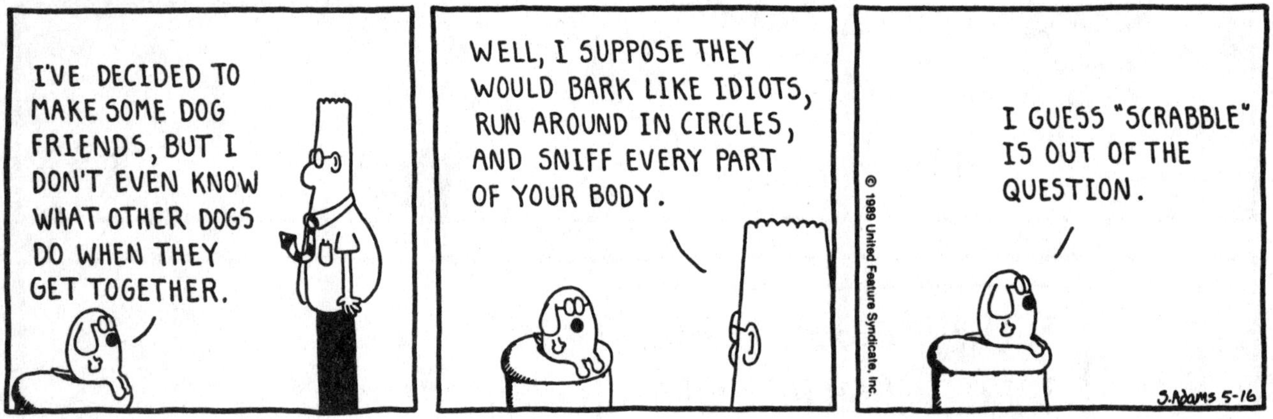
I'VE DECIDED TO MAKE SOME DOG FRIENDS, BUT I DON'T EVEN KNOW WHAT OTHER DOGS DO WHEN THEY GET TOGETHER.
WELL, I SUPPOSE THEY WOULD BARK LIKE IDIOTS, RUN AROUND IN CIRCLES, AND SNIFF EVERY PART OF YOUR BODY.
© 1989 United Feature Syndicate, Inc.
I GUESS "SCRABBLE" IS OUT OF THE QUESTION.
S.Adams 5-16

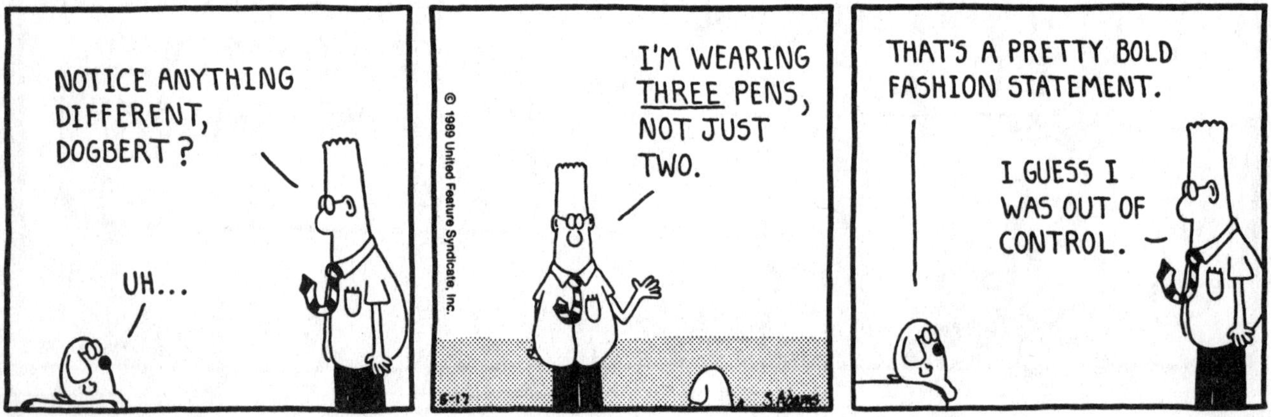
NOTICE ANYTHING DIFFERENT, DOGBERT?
UH...
© 1989 United Feature Syndicate, Inc.
I'M WEARING THREE PENS, NOT JUST TWO.
5-17
S.Adams
THAT'S A PRETTY BOLD FASHION STATEMENT.
I GUESS I WAS OUT OF CONTROL.

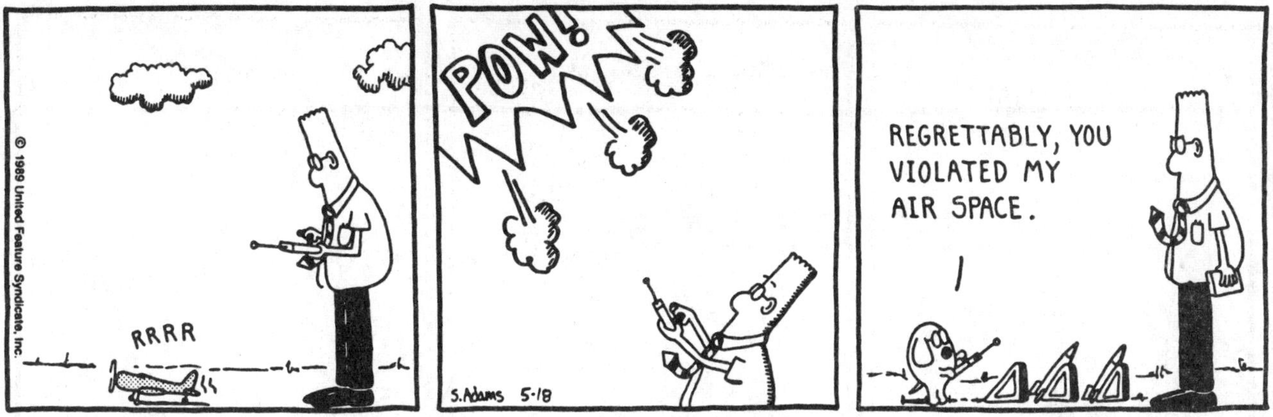
© 1989 United Feature Syndicate, Inc.
RRRR
POW!
S. Adams 5-18
REGRETTABLY, YOU VIOLATED MY AIR SPACE.

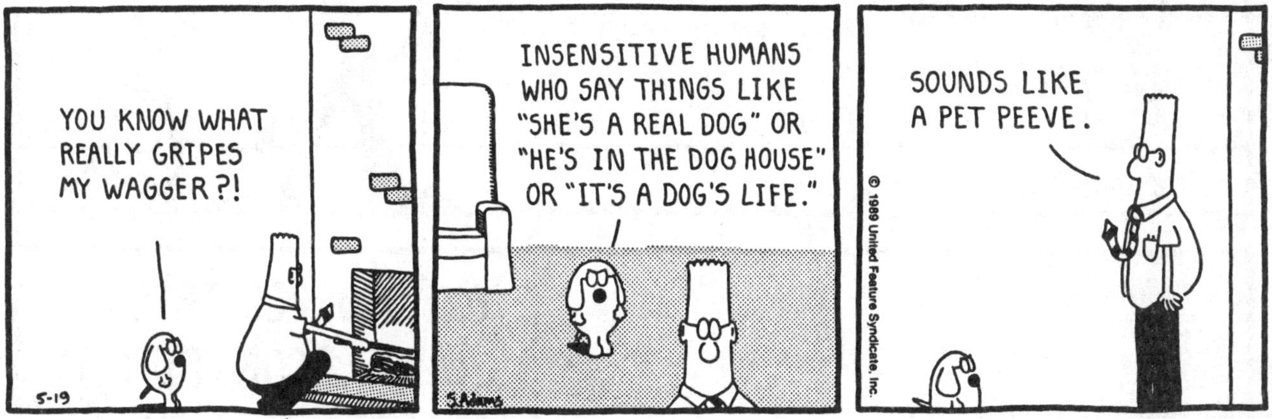
YOU KNOW WHAT REALLY GRIPES MY WAGGER?!
5-19
INSENSITIVE HUMANS WHO SAY THINGS LIKE "SHE'S A REAL DOG" OR "HE'S IN THE DOG HOUSE" OR "IT'S A DOG'S LIFE."
S. Adams
© 1989 United Feature Syndicate, Inc.
SOUNDS LIKE A PET PEEVE.

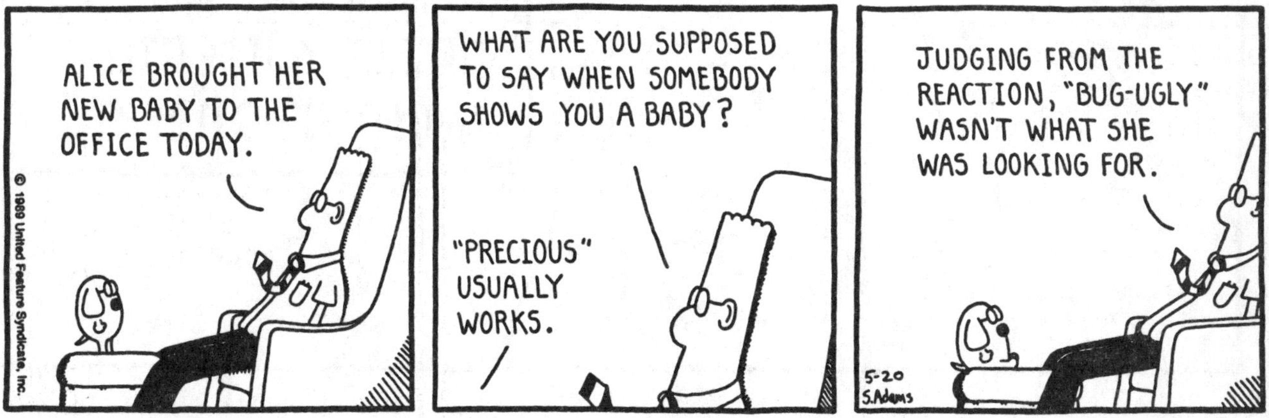
© 1989 United Feature Syndicate, Inc.
ALICE BROUGHT HER NEW BABY TO THE OFFICE TODAY.
WHAT ARE YOU SUPPOSED TO SAY WHEN SOMEBODY SHOWS YOU A BABY?
"PRECIOUS" USUALLY WORKS.
JUDGING FROM THE REACTION, "BUG-UGLY" WASN'T WHAT SHE WAS LOOKING FOR.
5-20
S. Adams

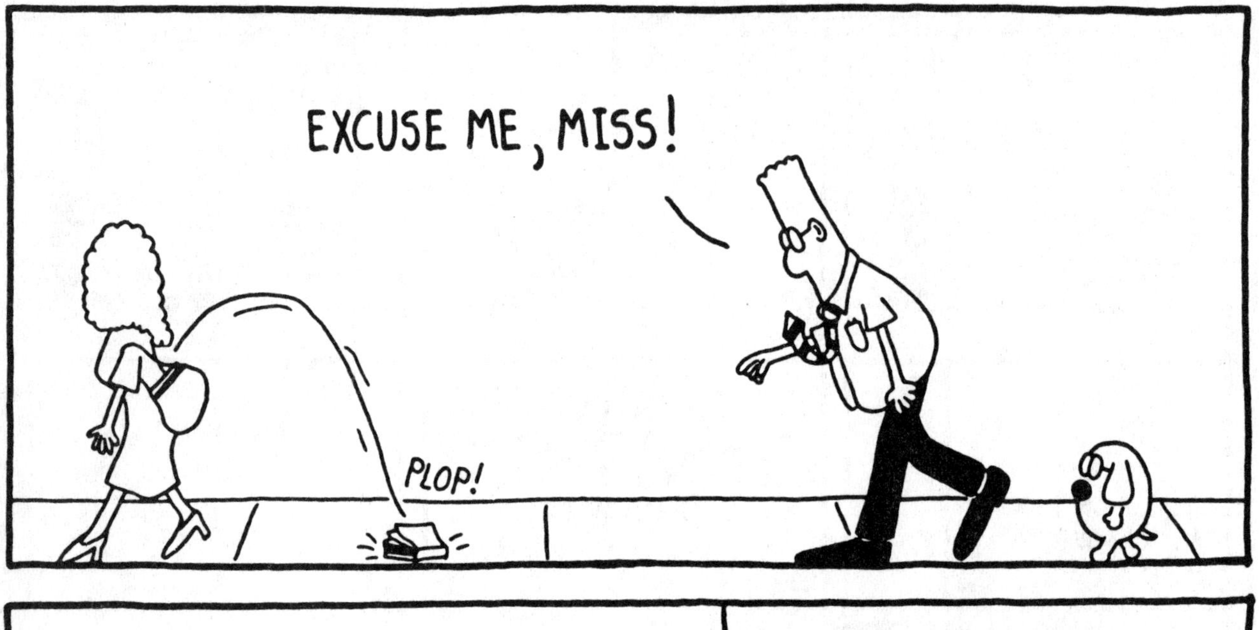
EXCUSE ME, MISS!
PLOP!
UH OH...
YOU DROPPED THIS LITTLE BOOK TITLED "ATTRACTIVE WOMEN'S SECRET GUIDE TO AVOIDING DILBERT."

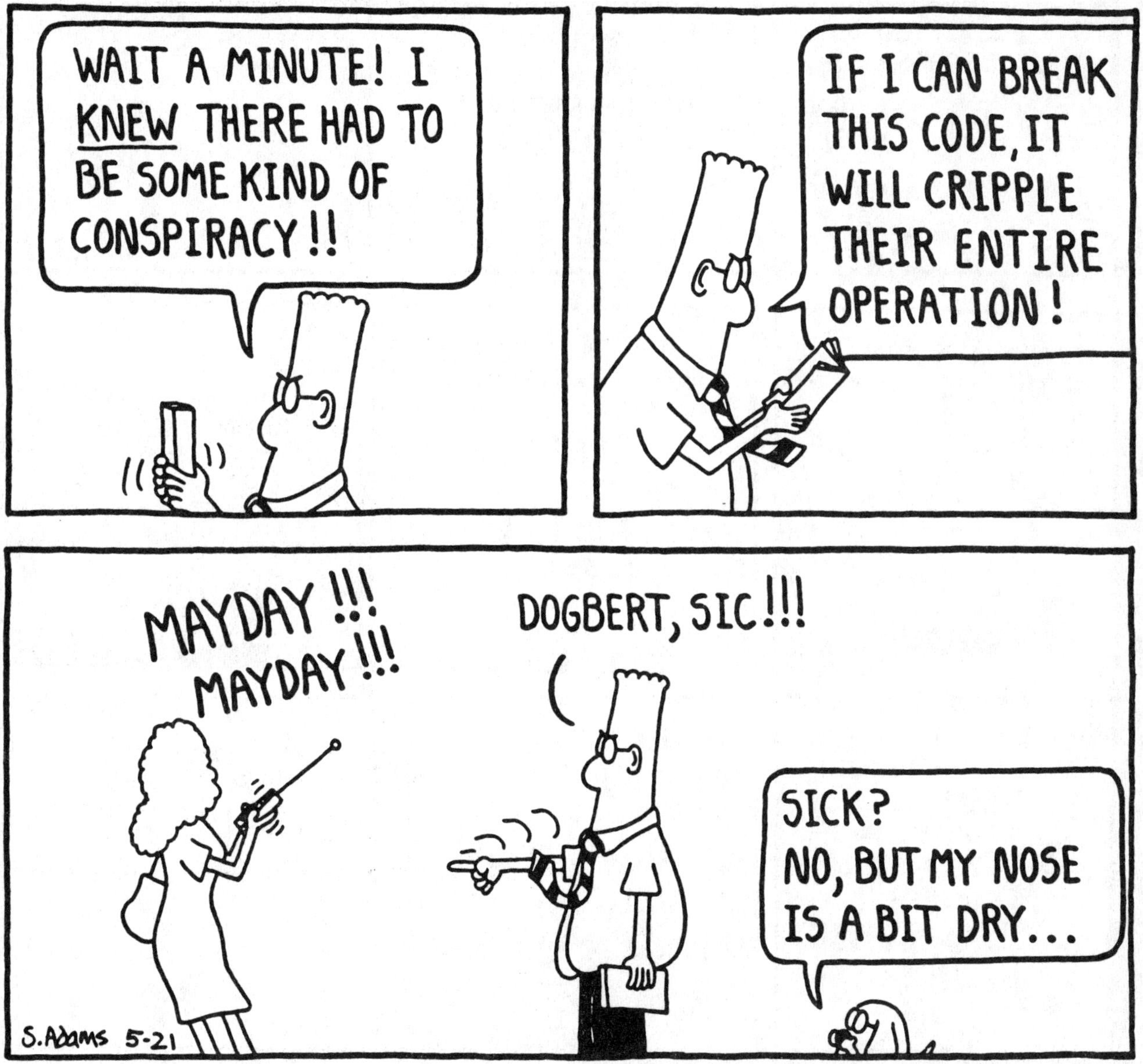
WAIT A MINUTE! I KNEW THERE HAD TO BE SOME KIND OF CONSPIRACY!!
IF I CAN BREAK THIS CODE, IT WILL CRIPPLE THEIR ENTIRE OPERATION!
MAYDAY!!! MAYDAY!!!
DOGBERT, SIC!!!
SICK? NO, BUT MY NOSE IS A BIT DRY...
S. Adams 5-21

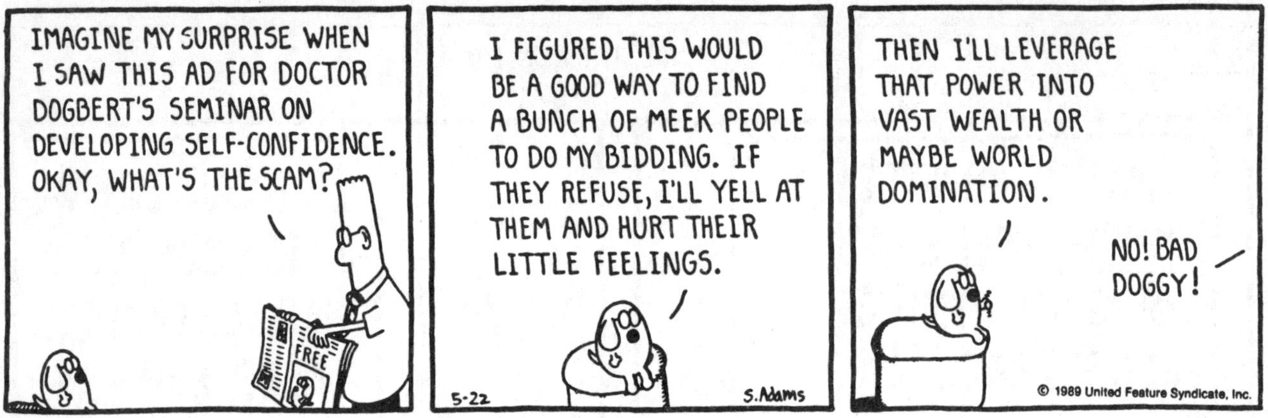
IMAGINE MY SURPRISE WHEN I SAW THIS AD FOR DOCTOR DOGBERT'S SEMINAR ON DEVELOPING SELF-CONFIDENCE. OKAY, WHAT'S THE SCAM?
FREE
I FIGURED THIS WOULD BE A GOOD WAY TO FIND A BUNCH OF MEEK PEOPLE TO DO MY BIDDING. IF THEY REFUSE, I'LL YELL AT THEM AND HURT THEIR LITTLE FEELINGS.
5-22
S.Adams
THEN I'LL LEVERAGE THAT POWER INTO VAST WEALTH OR MAYBE WORLD DOMINATION.
NO! BAD DOGGY!
© 1989 United Feature Syndicate, Inc.

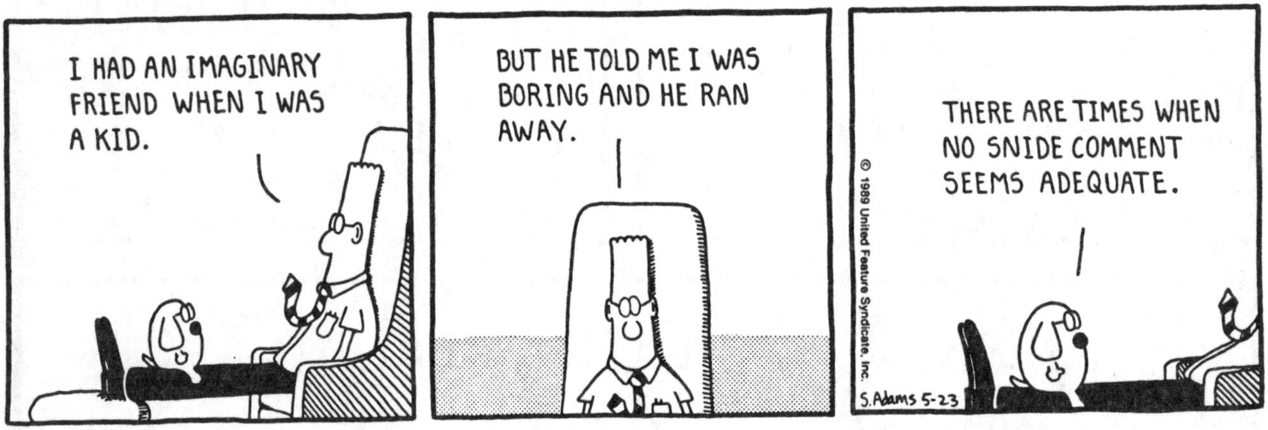
I HAD AN IMAGINARY FRIEND WHEN I WAS A KID.
BUT HE TOLD ME I WAS BORING AND HE RAN AWAY.
© 1989 United Feature Syndicate, Inc.
THERE ARE TIMES WHEN NO SNIDE COMMENT SEEMS ADEQUATE.
S.Adams 5-23

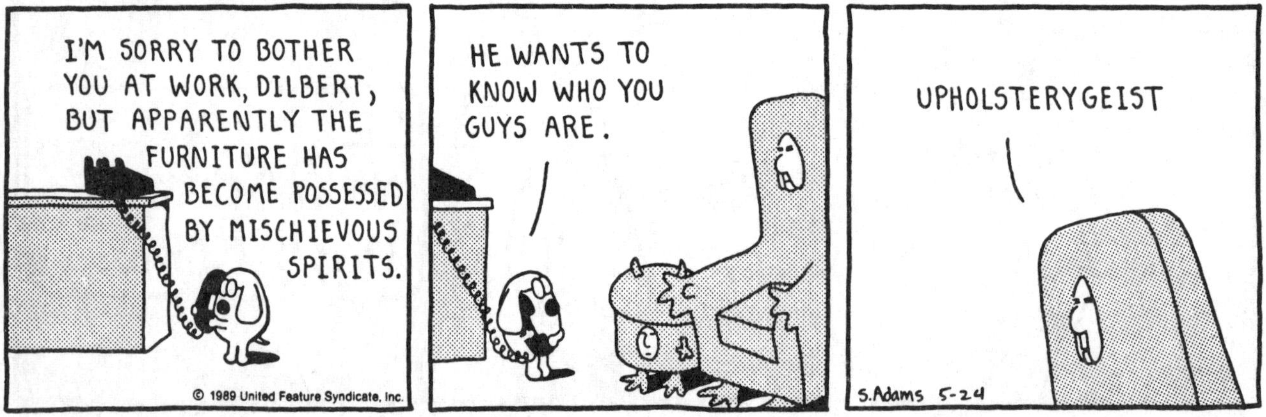
I'M SORRY TO BOTHER YOU AT WORK, DILBERT, BUT APPARENTLY THE FURNITURE HAS BECOME POSSESSED BY MISCHIEVOUS SPIRITS.
© 1989 United Feature Syndicate, Inc.
HE WANTS TO KNOW WHO YOU GUYS ARE.
UPHOLSTERYGEIST
S.Adams 5-24

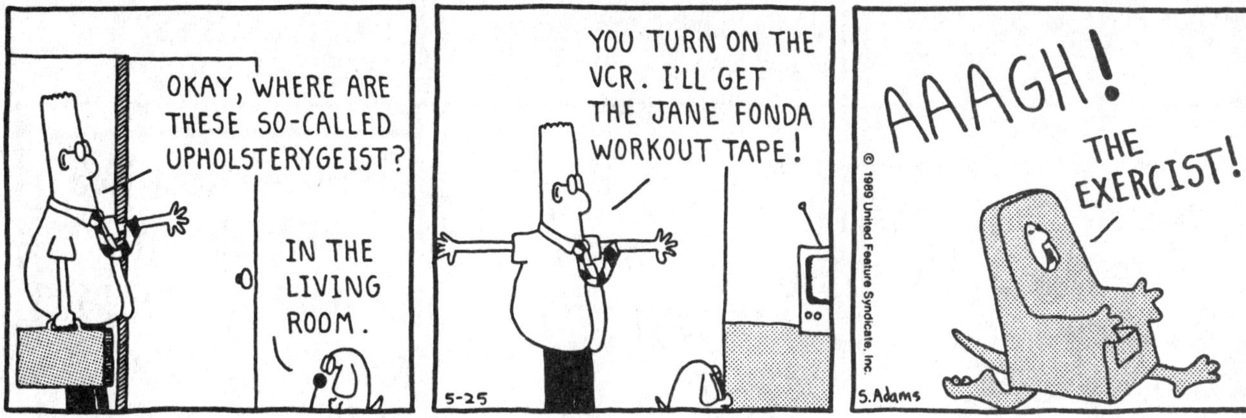
OKAY, WHERE ARE THESE SO-CALLED UPHOLSTERYGEIST?
IN THE LIVING ROOM.
5-25
YOU TURN ON THE VCR. I'LL GET THE JANE FONDA WORKOUT TAPE!
© 1989 United Feature Syndicate, Inc.
S. Adams
AAAGH!
THE EXERCIST!

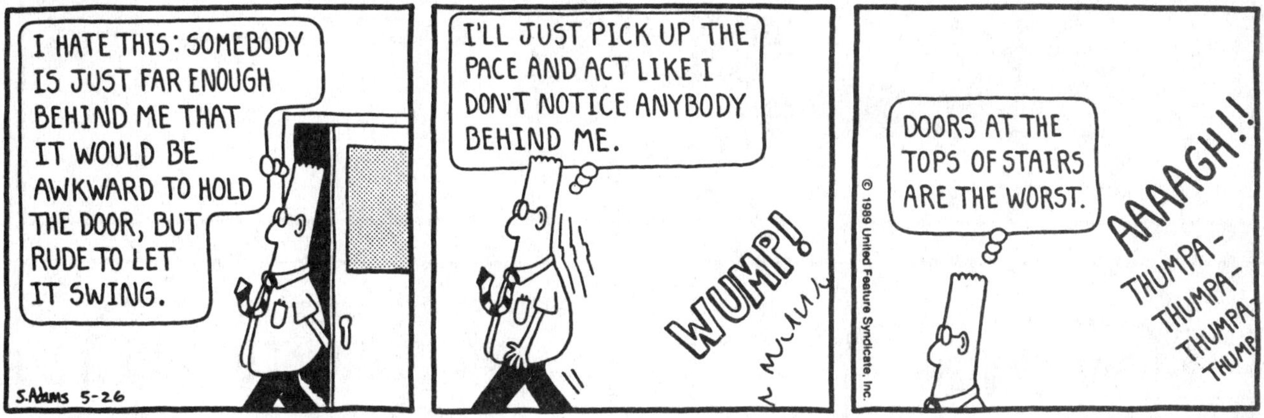
I HATE THIS: SOMEBODY IS JUST FAR ENOUGH BEHIND ME THAT IT WOULD BE AWKWARD TO HOLD THE DOOR, BUT RUDE TO LET IT SWING.
S. Adams 5-26
I'LL JUST PICK UP THE PACE AND ACT LIKE I DON'T NOTICE ANYBODY BEHIND ME.
WUMP!
© 1989 United Feature Syndicate, Inc.
DOORS AT THE TOPS OF STAIRS ARE THE WORST.
AAAAGH!!
THUMPA-
THUMPA-
THUMPA-
THUMP

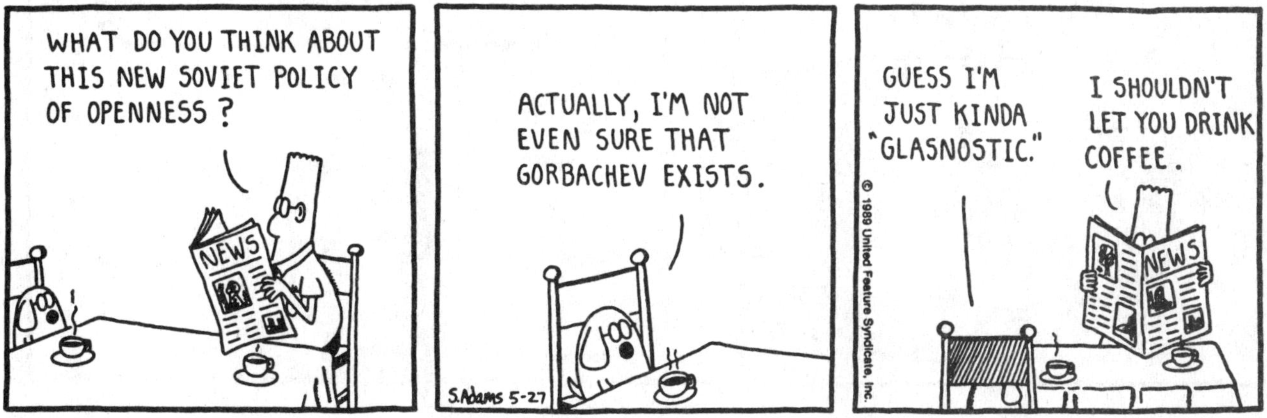
WHAT DO YOU THINK ABOUT THIS NEW SOVIET POLICY OF OPENNESS?
NEWS
ACTUALLY, I'M NOT EVEN SURE THAT GORBACHEV EXISTS.
S. Adams 5-27
© 1989 United Feature Syndicate, Inc.
GUESS I'M JUST KINDA "GLASNOSTIC."
I SHOULDN'T LET YOU DRINK COFFEE.
NEWS

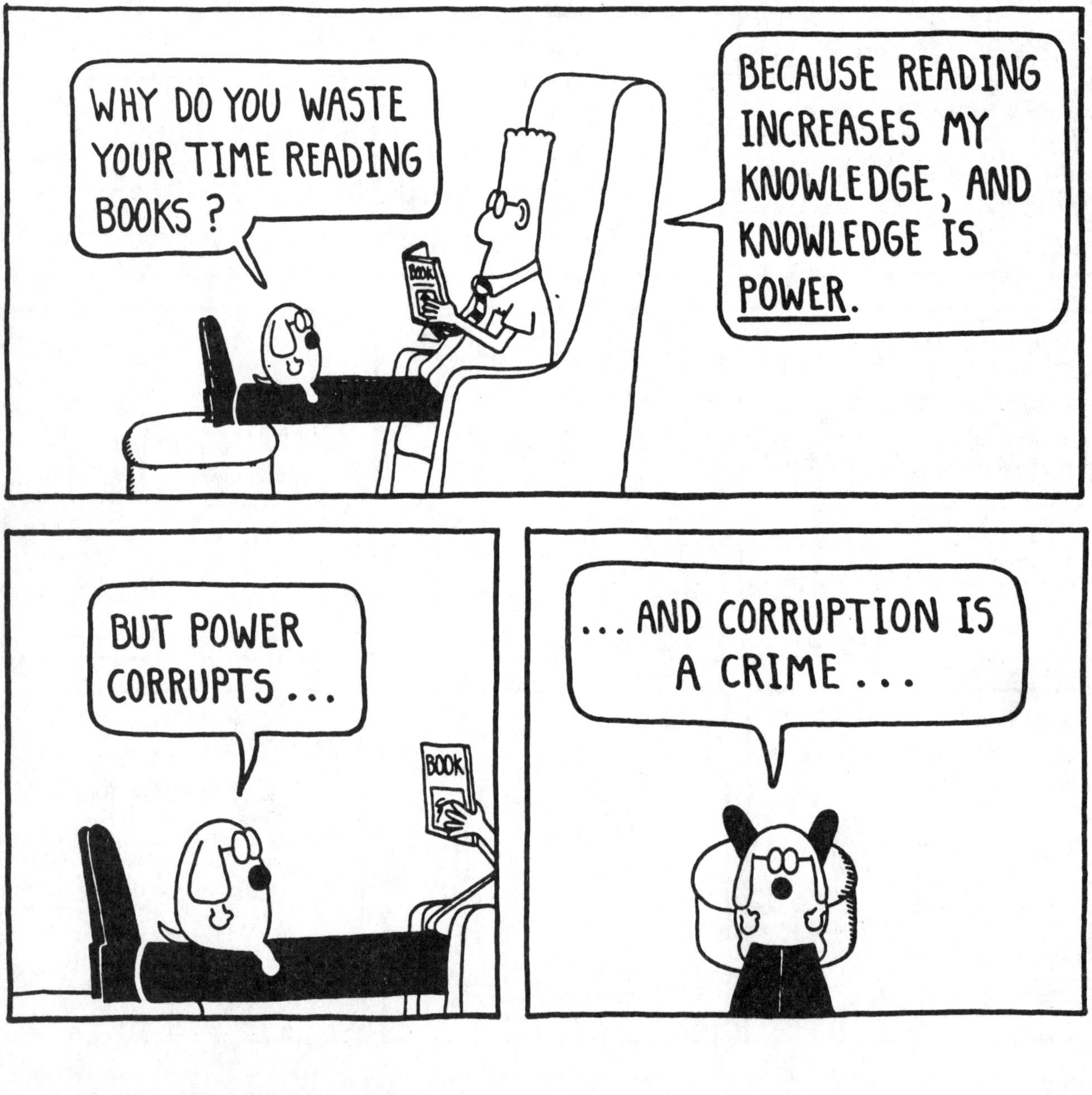
WHY DO YOU WASTE YOUR TIME READING BOOKS ?
BOOK
BECAUSE READING INCREASES MY KNOWLEDGE, AND KNOWLEDGE IS POWER.
BUT POWER CORRUPTS . . .
BOOK
. . . AND CORRUPTION IS A CRIME . . .

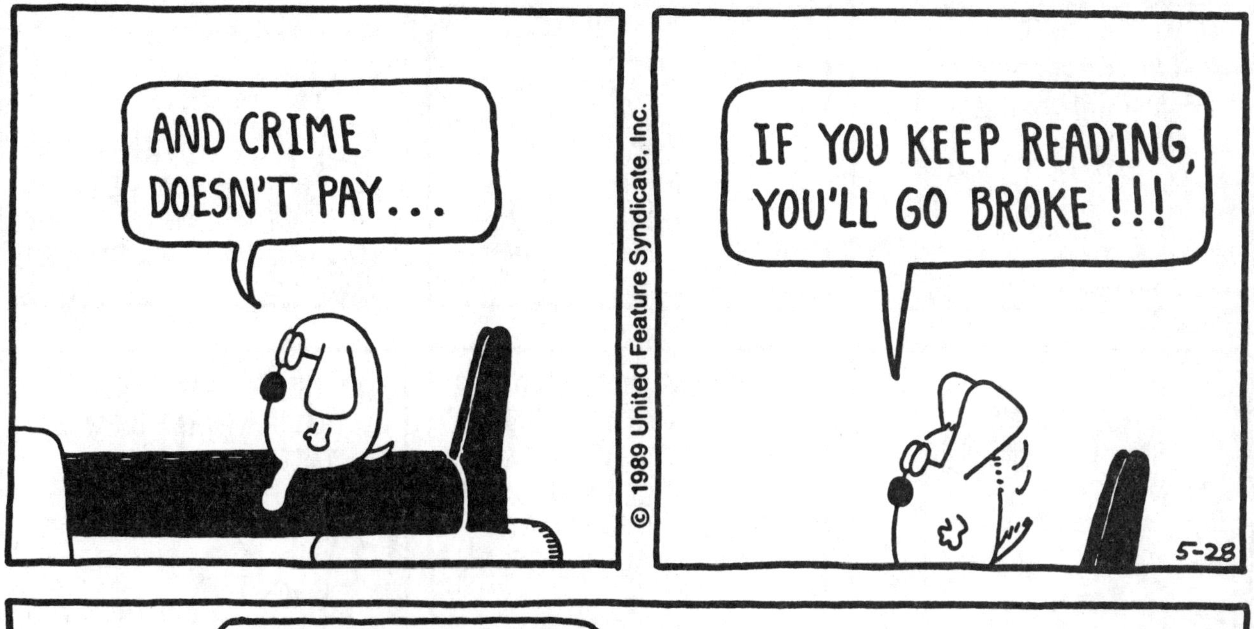
AND CRIME DOESN'T PAY...
© 1989 United Feature Syndicate, Inc.
IF YOU KEEP READING, YOU'LL GO BROKE !!!
5-28
GOSH! IT ALWAYS SEEMED SO...SO ...HARMLESS.
OH YEAH, THE LIBRARIANS WOULD LOVE TO HAVE YOU BELIEVE THAT!
S.Adams

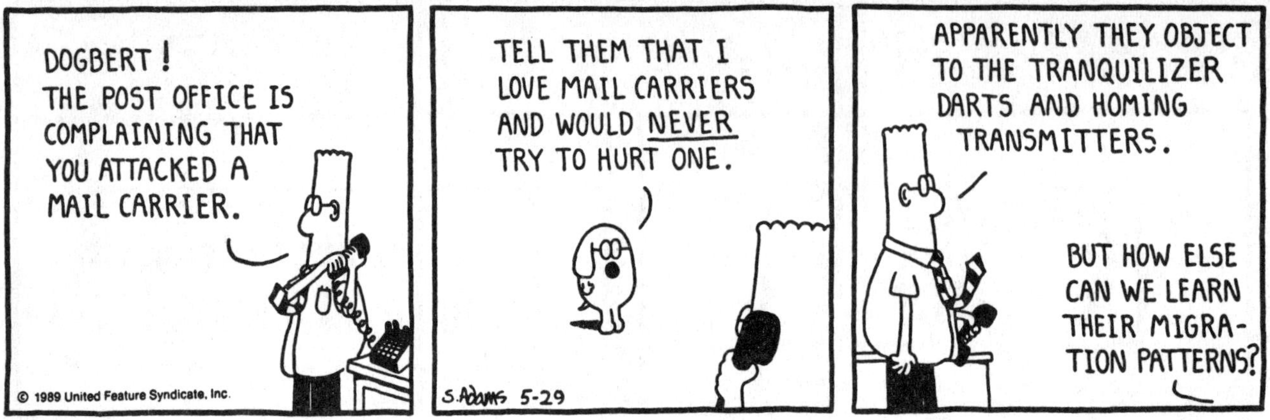
DOGBERT! THE POST OFFICE IS COMPLAINING THAT YOU ATTACKED A MAIL CARRIER.
© 1989 United Feature Syndicate, Inc.
TELL THEM THAT I LOVE MAIL CARRIERS AND WOULD NEVER TRY TO HURT ONE.
S. Adams 5-29
APPARENTLY THEY OBJECT TO THE TRANQUILIZER DARTS AND HOMING TRANSMITTERS.
BUT HOW ELSE CAN WE LEARN THEIR MIGRATION PATTERNS?

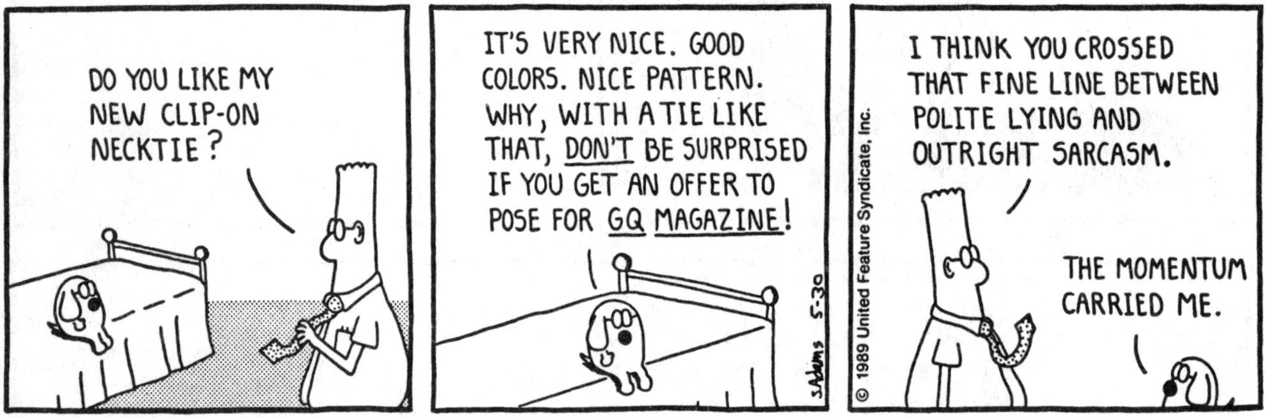
DO YOU LIKE MY NEW CLIP-ON NECKTIE?
IT'S VERY NICE. GOOD COLORS. NICE PATTERN. WHY, WITH A TIE LIKE THAT, DON'T BE SURPRISED IF YOU GET AN OFFER TO POSE FOR GQ MAGAZINE!
S. Adams 5-30
© 1989 United Feature Syndicate, Inc.
I THINK YOU CROSSED THAT FINE LINE BETWEEN POLITE LYING AND OUTRIGHT SARCASM.
THE MOMENTUM CARRIED ME.

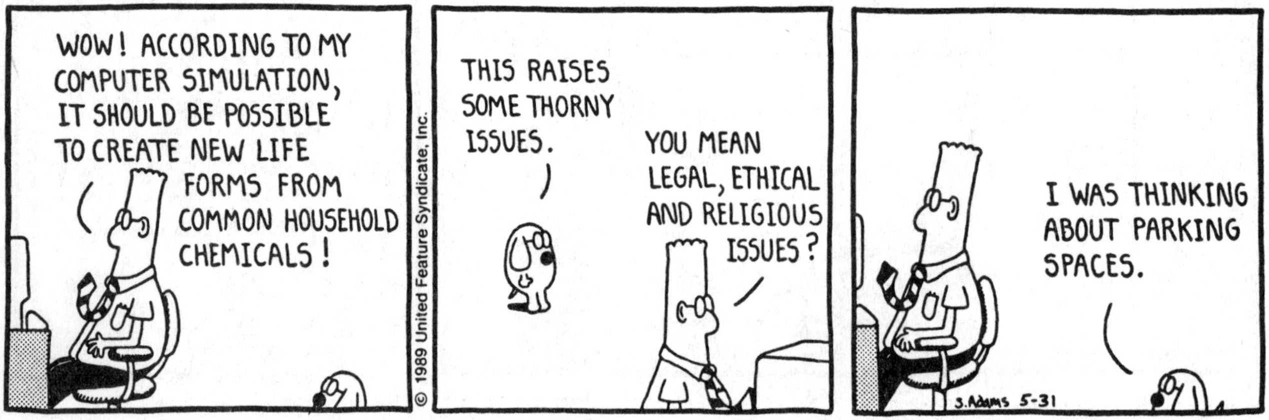
WOW! ACCORDING TO MY COMPUTER SIMULATION, IT SHOULD BE POSSIBLE TO CREATE NEW LIFE FORMS FROM COMMON HOUSEHOLD CHEMICALS!
© 1989 United Feature Syndicate, Inc.
THIS RAISES SOME THORNY ISSUES.
YOU MEAN LEGAL, ETHICAL AND RELIGIOUS ISSUES?
I WAS THINKING ABOUT PARKING SPACES.
S. Adams 5-31

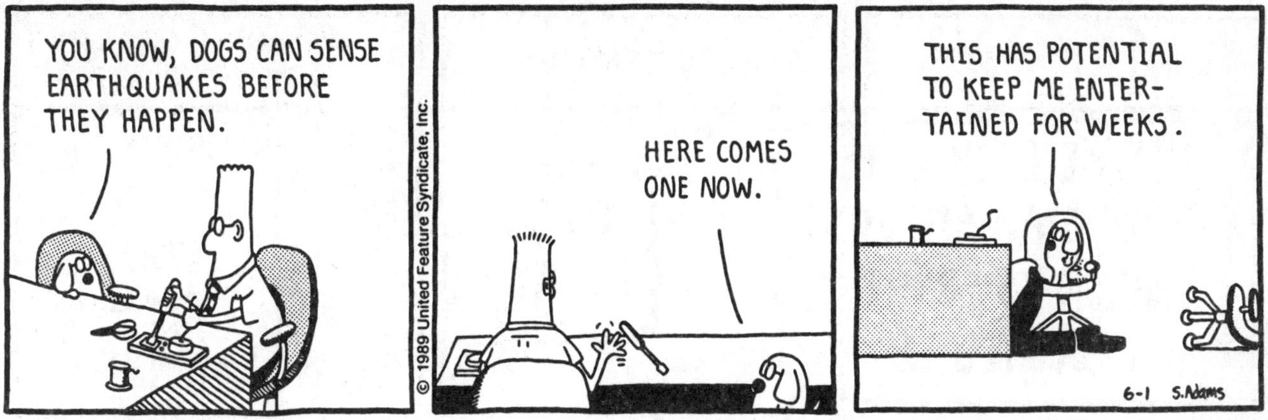
YOU KNOW, DOGS CAN SENSE EARTHQUAKES BEFORE THEY HAPPEN.
© 1989 United Feature Syndicate, Inc.
HERE COMES ONE NOW.
THIS HAS POTENTIAL TO KEEP ME ENTERTAINED FOR WEEKS.
6-1 S.Adams

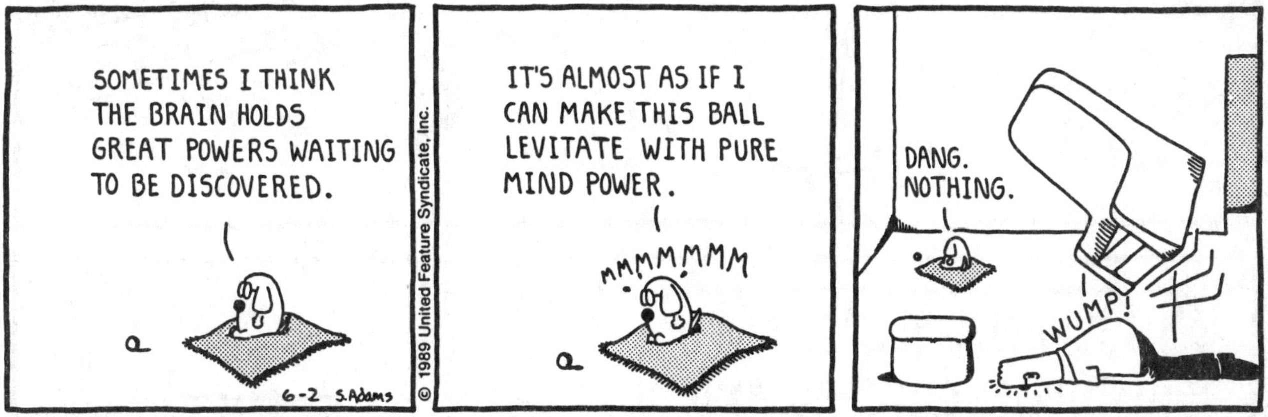
SOMETIMES I THINK THE BRAIN HOLDS GREAT POWERS WAITING TO BE DISCOVERED.
6-2 S.Adams
© 1989 United Feature Syndicate, Inc.
IT'S ALMOST AS IF I CAN MAKE THIS BALL LEVITATE WITH PURE MIND POWER.
MMMMMMM
DANG. NOTHING.
WUMP!

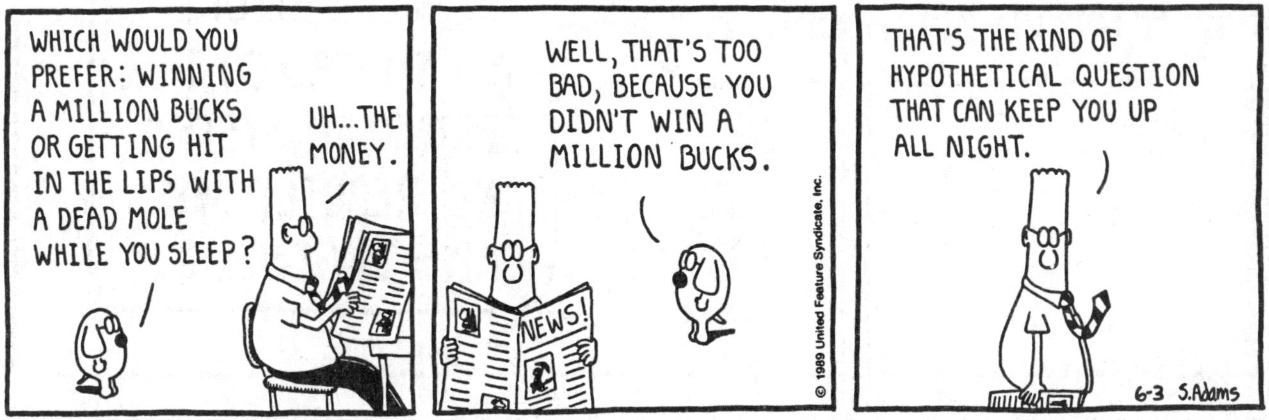
WHICH WOULD YOU PREFER: WINNING A MILLION BUCKS OR GETTING HIT IN THE LIPS WITH A DEAD MOLE WHILE YOU SLEEP?
UH...THE MONEY.
WELL, THAT'S TOO BAD, BECAUSE YOU DIDN'T WIN A MILLION BUCKS.
NEWS!
© 1989 United Feature Syndicate, Inc.
THAT'S THE KIND OF HYPOTHETICAL QUESTION THAT CAN KEEP YOU UP ALL NIGHT.
6-3 S.Adams

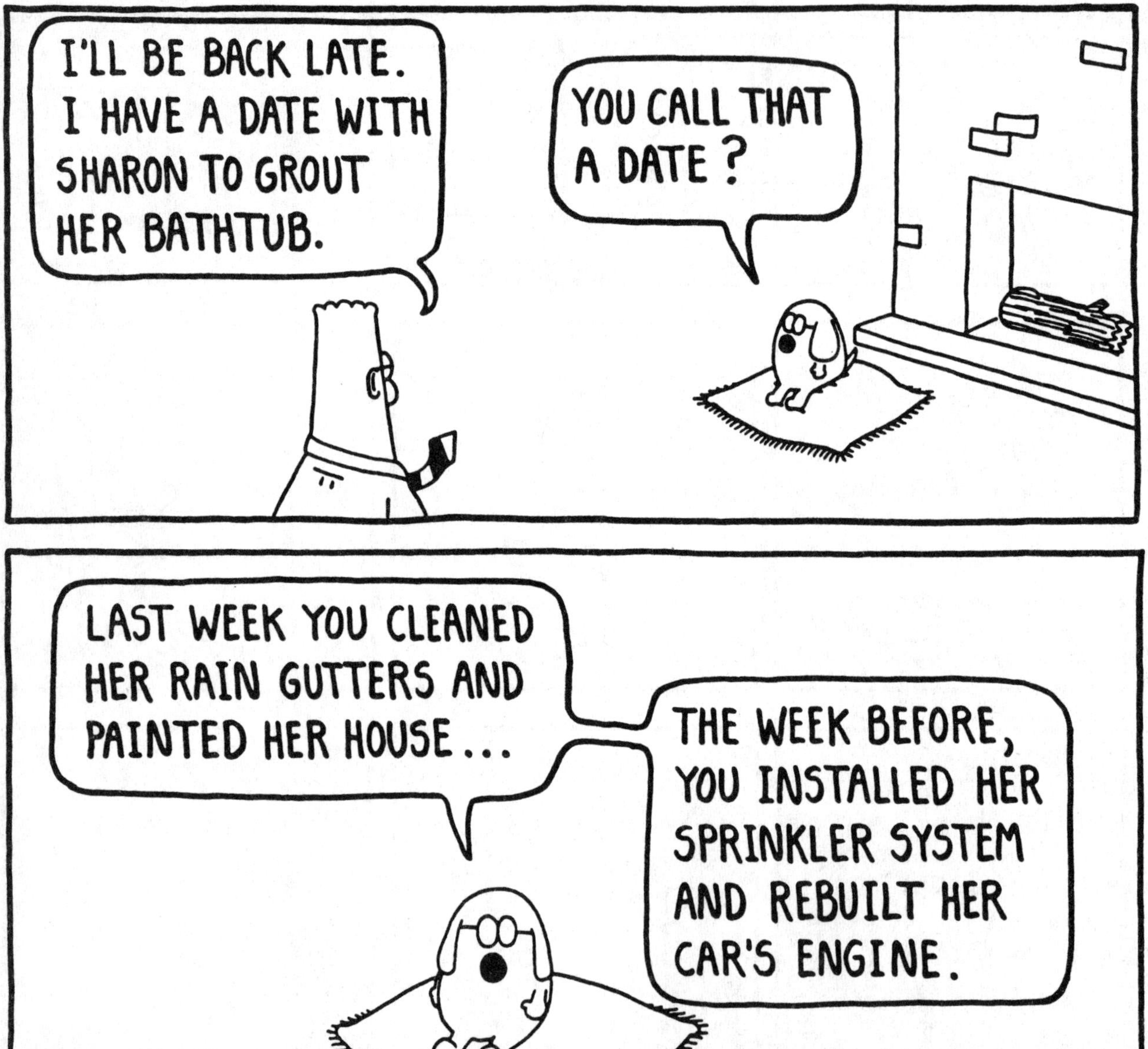
I'LL BE BACK LATE. I HAVE A DATE WITH SHARON TO GROUT HER BATHTUB.
YOU CALL THAT A DATE?
LAST WEEK YOU CLEANED HER RAIN GUTTERS AND PAINTED HER HOUSE...
THE WEEK BEFORE, YOU INSTALLED HER SPRINKLER SYSTEM AND REBUILT HER CAR'S ENGINE.

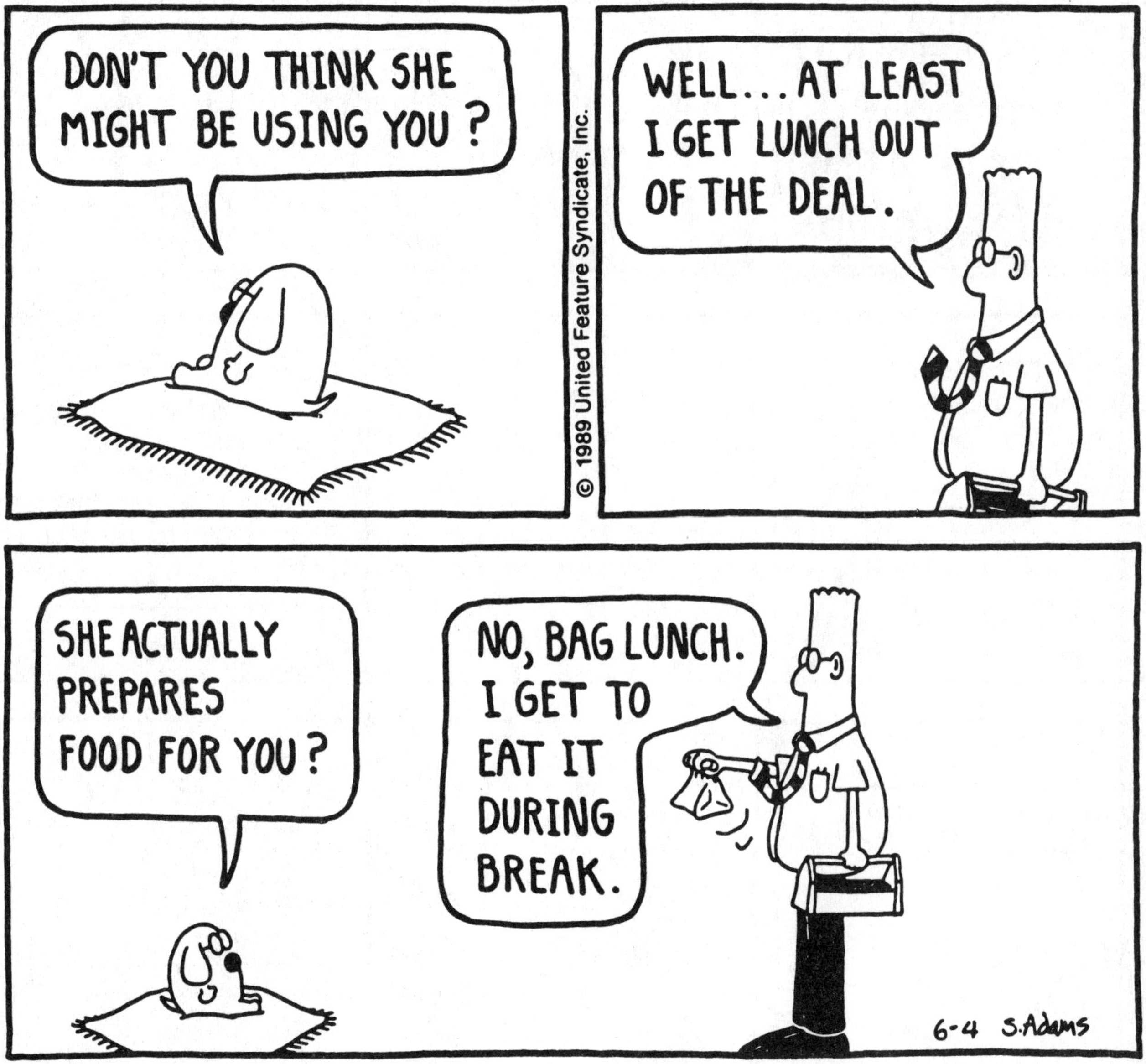
DON'T YOU THINK SHE MIGHT BE USING YOU?
© 1989 United Feature Syndicate, Inc.
WELL... AT LEAST I GET LUNCH OUT OF THE DEAL.
SHE ACTUALLY PREPARES FOOD FOR YOU?
NO, BAG LUNCH. I GET TO EAT IT DURING BREAK.
6-4 S. Adams

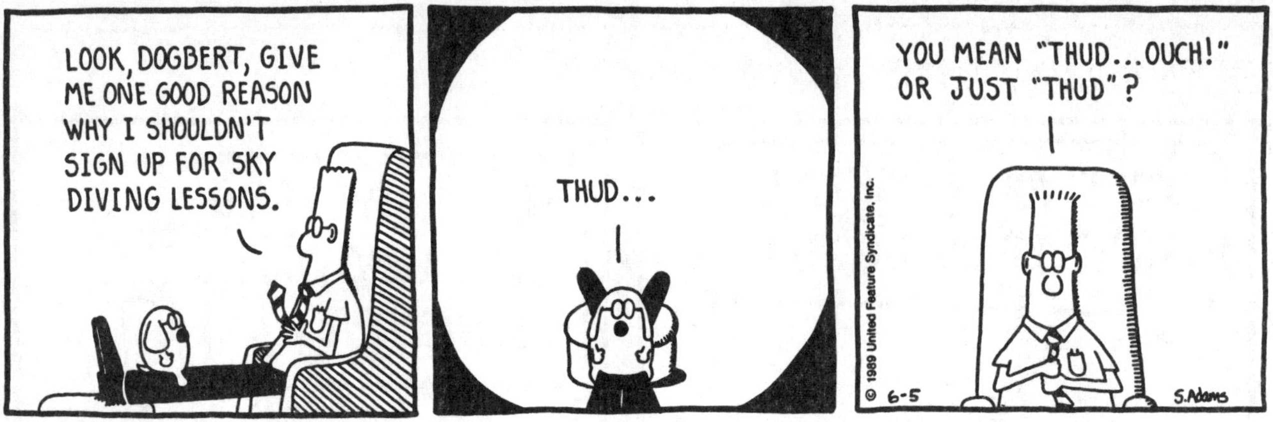
LOOK, DOGBERT, GIVE ME ONE GOOD REASON WHY I SHOULDN'T SIGN UP FOR SKY DIVING LESSONS.
THUD...
YOU MEAN "THUD...OUCH!" OR JUST "THUD"?
© 1989 United Feature Syndicate, Inc.
6-5
S.Adams

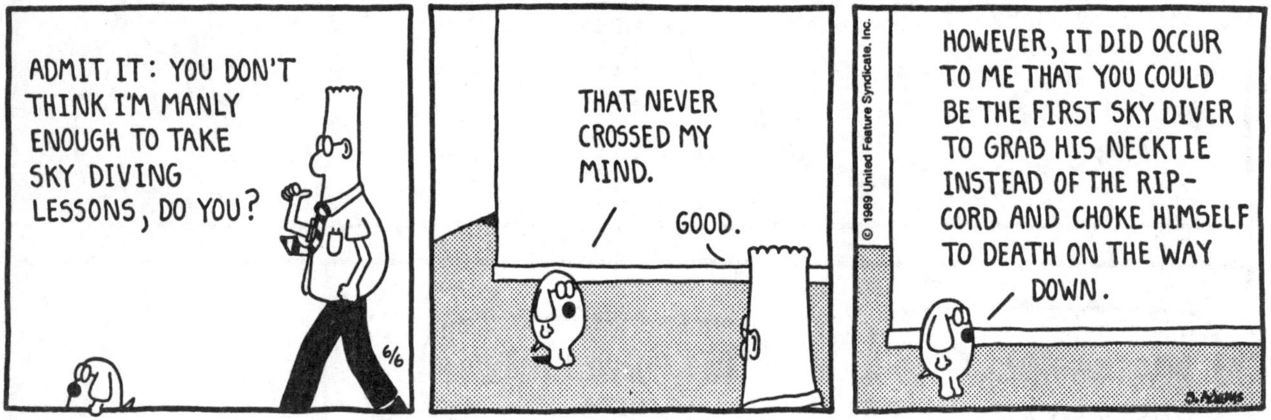
ADMIT IT: YOU DON'T THINK I'M MANLY ENOUGH TO TAKE SKY DIVING LESSONS, DO YOU?
6/6
THAT NEVER CROSSED MY MIND.
GOOD.
© 1989 United Feature Syndicate, Inc.
HOWEVER, IT DID OCCUR TO ME THAT YOU COULD BE THE FIRST SKY DIVER TO GRAB HIS NECKTIE INSTEAD OF THE RIP-CORD AND CHOKE HIMSELF TO DEATH ON THE WAY DOWN.
S.Adams

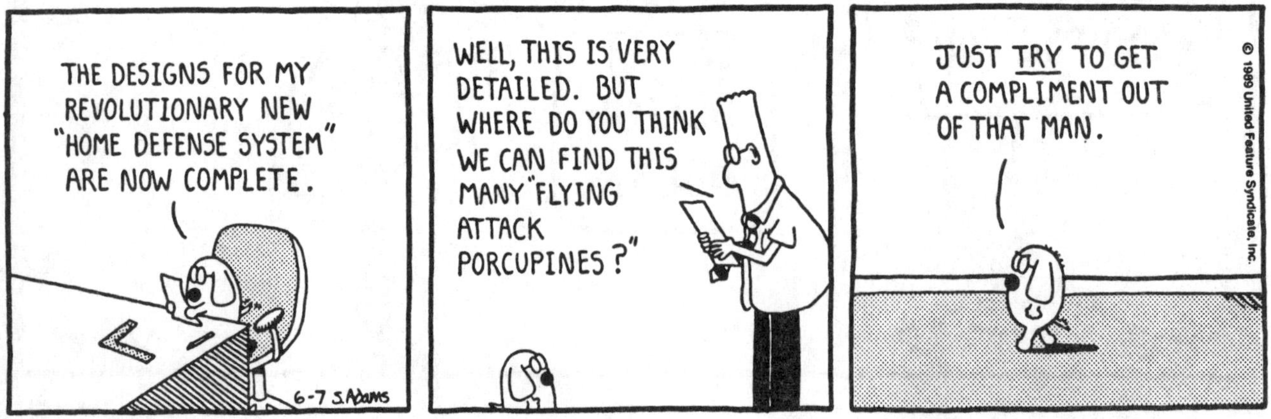
THE DESIGNS FOR MY REVOLUTIONARY NEW "HOME DEFENSE SYSTEM" ARE NOW COMPLETE.
6-7 S.Adams
WELL, THIS IS VERY DETAILED. BUT WHERE DO YOU THINK WE CAN FIND THIS MANY "FLYING ATTACK PORCUPINES?"
JUST TRY TO GET A COMPLIMENT OUT OF THAT MAN.
© 1989 United Feature Syndicate, Inc.

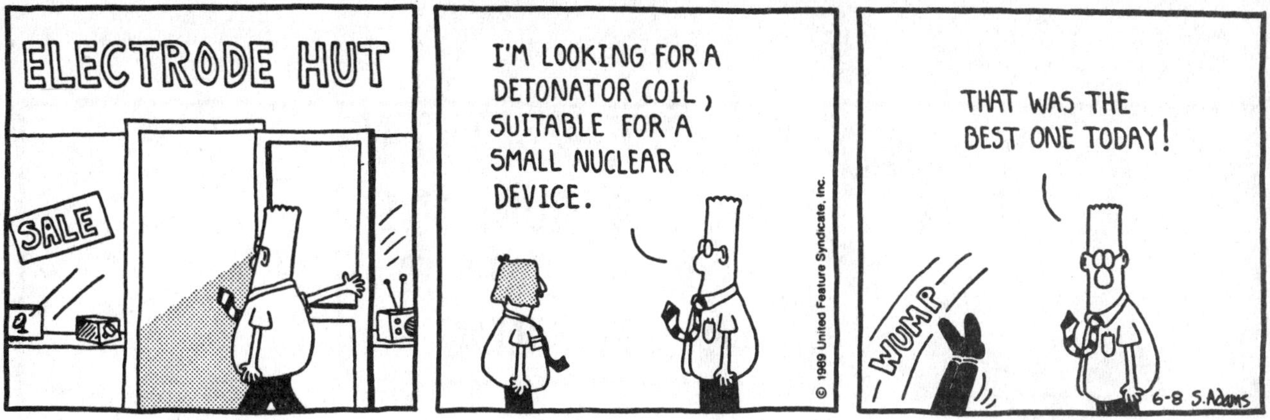
ELECTRODE HUT
SALE
I'M LOOKING FOR A DETONATOR COIL, SUITABLE FOR A SMALL NUCLEAR DEVICE.
© 1989 United Feature Syndicate, Inc.
THAT WAS THE BEST ONE TODAY!
WUMP
6-8 S.Adams

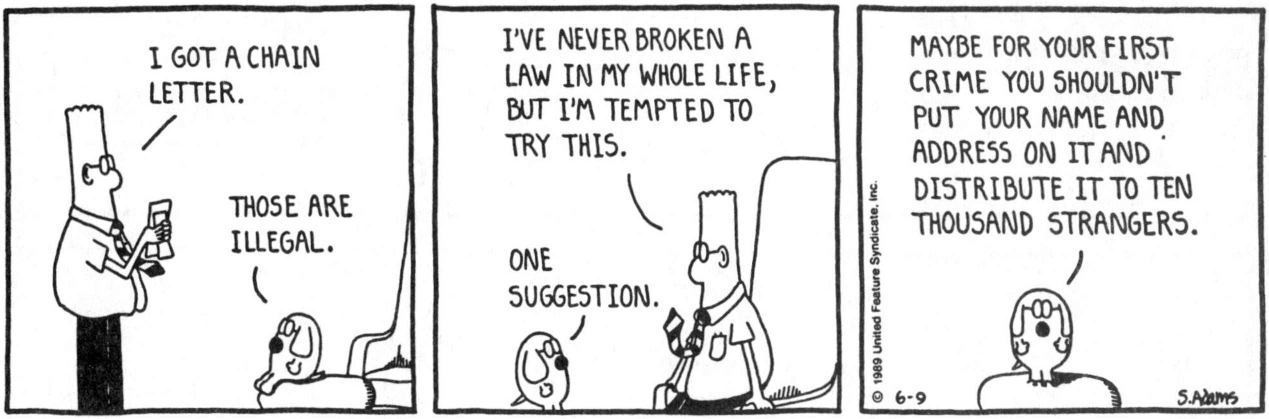
I GOT A CHAIN LETTER.
THOSE ARE ILLEGAL.
I'VE NEVER BROKEN A LAW IN MY WHOLE LIFE, BUT I'M TEMPTED TO TRY THIS.
ONE SUGGESTION.
© 1989 United Feature Syndicate, Inc.
MAYBE FOR YOUR FIRST CRIME YOU SHOULDN'T PUT YOUR NAME AND ADDRESS ON IT AND DISTRIBUTE IT TO TEN THOUSAND STRANGERS.
6-9
S.Adams

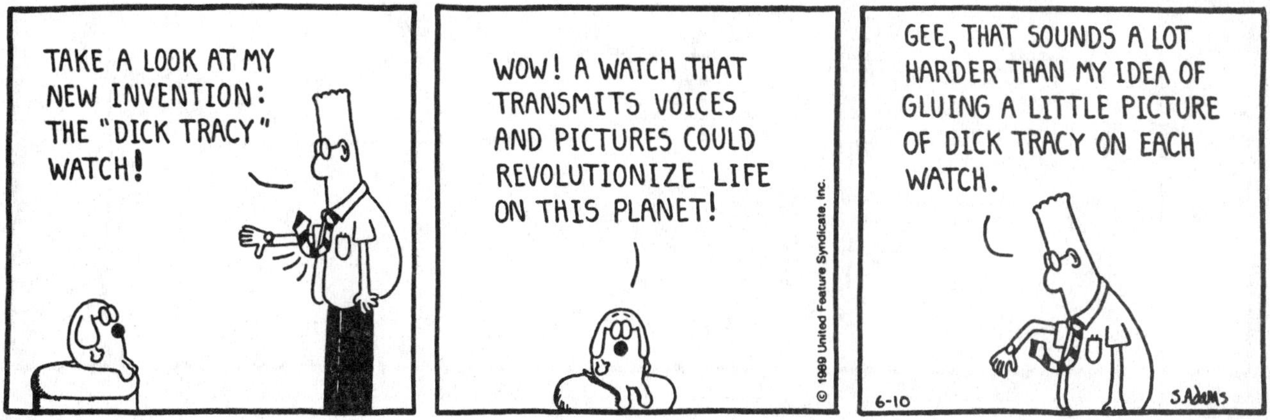
TAKE A LOOK AT MY NEW INVENTION: THE "DICK TRACY" WATCH!
WOW! A WATCH THAT TRANSMITS VOICES AND PICTURES COULD REVOLUTIONIZE LIFE ON THIS PLANET!
© 1989 United Feature Syndicate, Inc.
GEE, THAT SOUNDS A LOT HARDER THAN MY IDEA OF GLUING A LITTLE PICTURE OF DICK TRACY ON EACH WATCH.
6-10
S.Adams

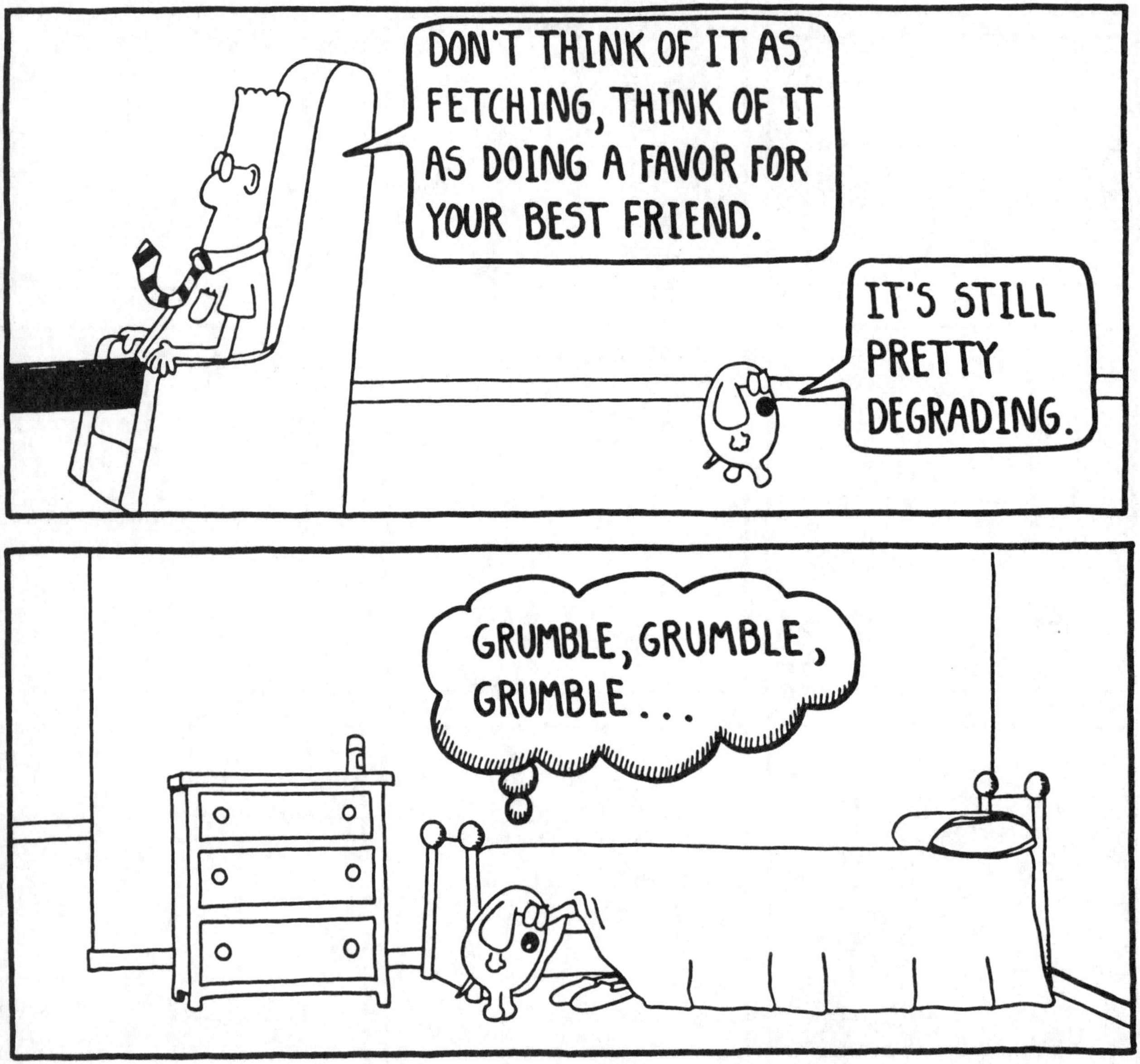
DON'T THINK OF IT AS FETCHING, THINK OF IT AS DOING A FAVOR FOR YOUR BEST FRIEND.
IT'S STILL PRETTY DEGRADING.
GRUMBLE, GRUMBLE, GRUMBLE . . .

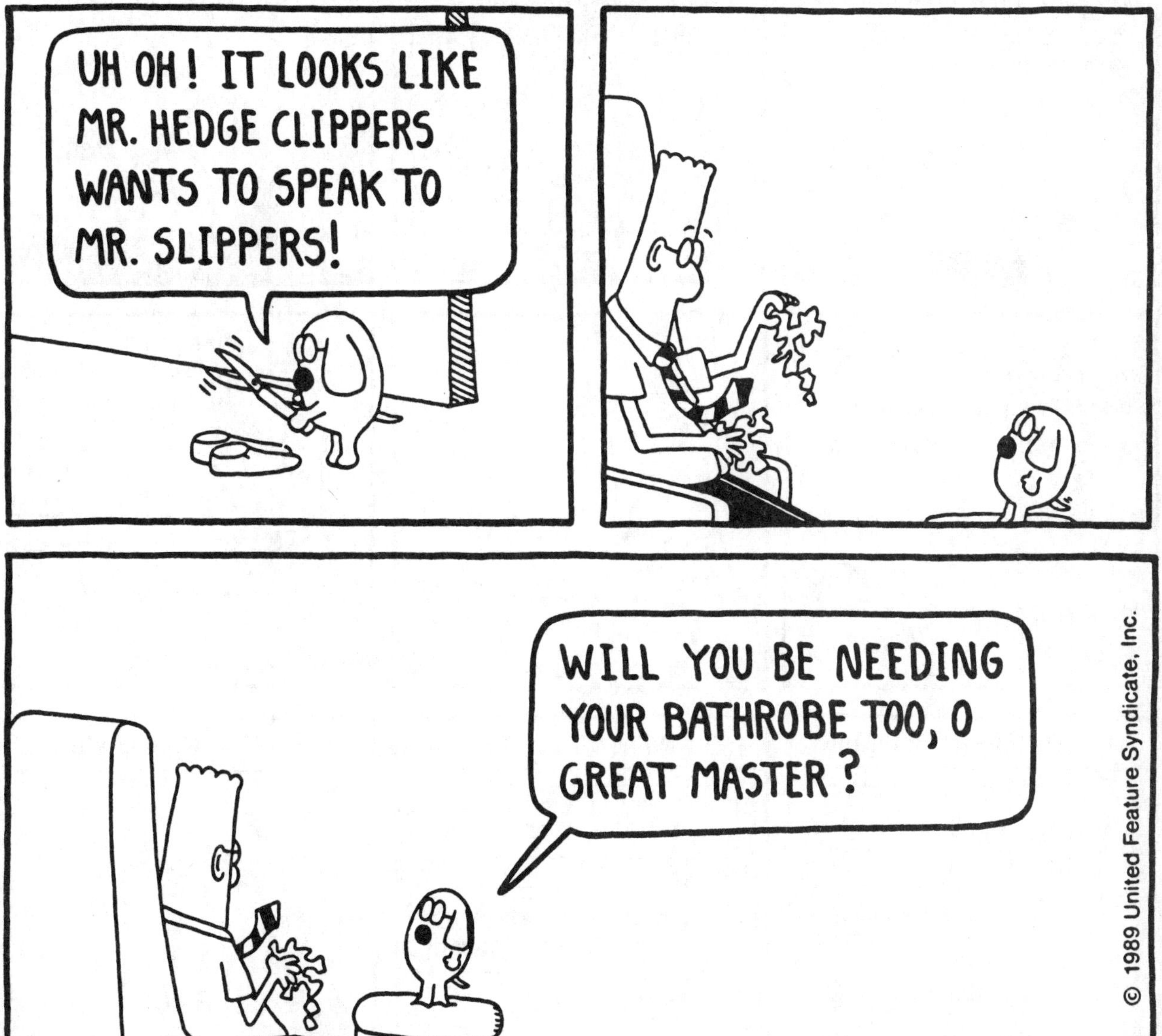
UH OH! IT LOOKS LIKE MR. HEDGE CLIPPERS WANTS TO SPEAK TO MR. SLIPPERS!
WILL YOU BE NEEDING YOUR BATHROBE TOO, O GREAT MASTER?
© 1989 United Feature Syndicate, Inc.
S. Adams 6-11

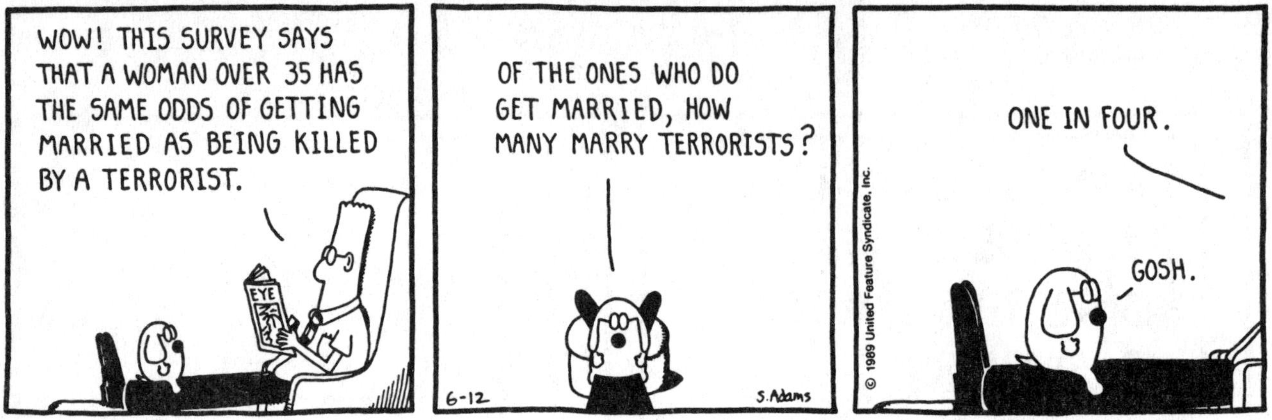
WOW! THIS SURVEY SAYS THAT A WOMAN OVER 35 HAS THE SAME ODDS OF GETTING MARRIED AS BEING KILLED BY A TERRORIST.
EYE
OF THE ONES WHO DO GET MARRIED, HOW MANY MARRY TERRORISTS?
6-12
S. Adams
ONE IN FOUR.
GOSH.
© 1989 United Feature Syndicate, Inc.

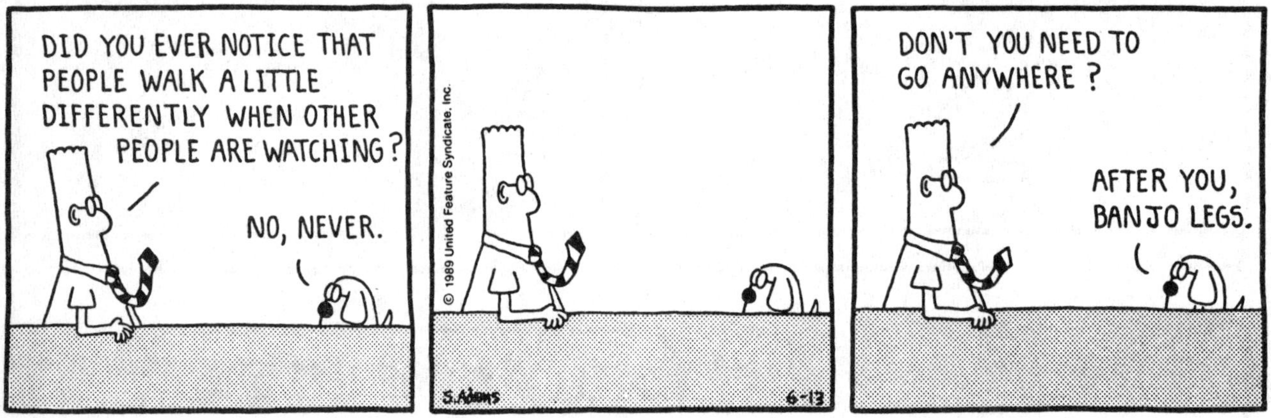
DID YOU EVER NOTICE THAT PEOPLE WALK A LITTLE DIFFERENTLY WHEN OTHER PEOPLE ARE WATCHING?
NO, NEVER.
© 1989 United Feature Syndicate, Inc.
S. Adams
6-13
DON'T YOU NEED TO GO ANYWHERE?
AFTER YOU, BANJO LEGS.

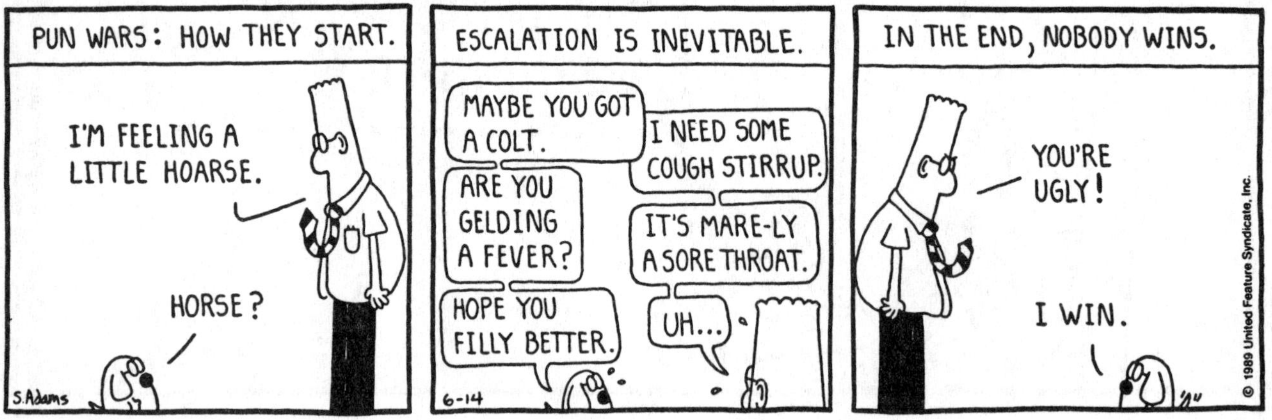
PUN WARS: HOW THEY START.
I'M FEELING A LITTLE HOARSE.
HORSE?
S. Adams
ESCALATION IS INEVITABLE.
MAYBE YOU GOT A COLT.
I NEED SOME COUGH STIRRUP.
ARE YOU GELDING A FEVER?
IT'S MARE-LY A SORE THROAT.
HOPE YOU FILLY BETTER.
UH...
6-14
IN THE END, NOBODY WINS.
YOU'RE UGLY!
I WIN.
© 1989 United Feature Syndicate, Inc.

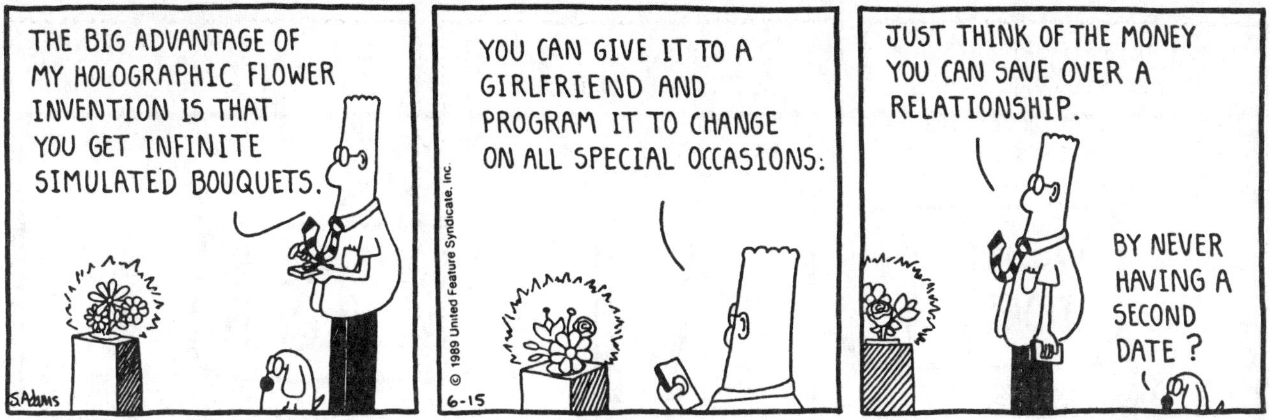
THE BIG ADVANTAGE OF MY HOLOGRAPHIC FLOWER INVENTION IS THAT YOU GET INFINITE SIMULATED BOUQUETS.
S.Adams
© 1989 United Feature Syndicate, Inc.
6-15
YOU CAN GIVE IT TO A GIRLFRIEND AND PROGRAM IT TO CHANGE ON ALL SPECIAL OCCASIONS.
JUST THINK OF THE MONEY YOU CAN SAVE OVER A RELATIONSHIP.
BY NEVER HAVING A SECOND DATE ?

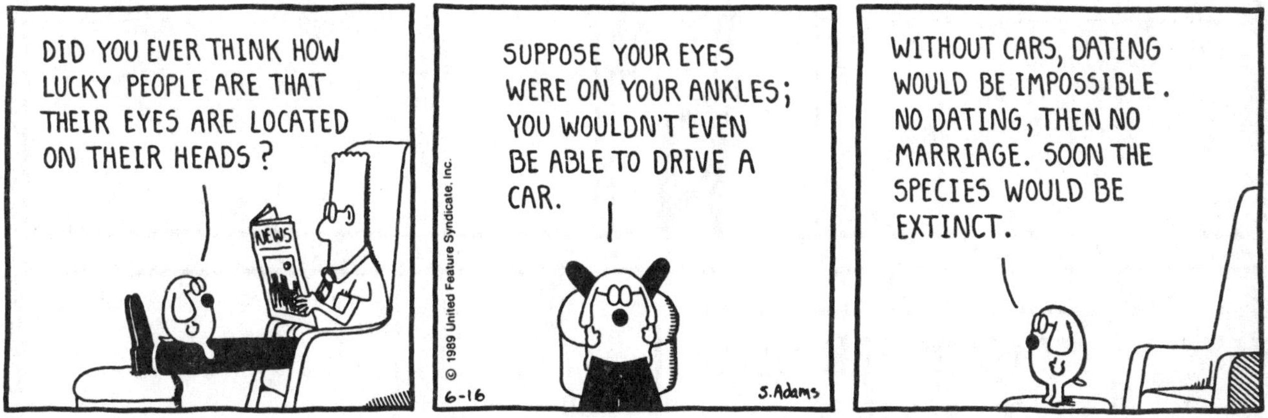
DID YOU EVER THINK HOW LUCKY PEOPLE ARE THAT THEIR EYES ARE LOCATED ON THEIR HEADS ?
NEWS
© 1989 United Feature Syndicate, Inc.
6-16
SUPPOSE YOUR EYES WERE ON YOUR ANKLES; YOU WOULDN'T EVEN BE ABLE TO DRIVE A CAR.
S.Adams
WITHOUT CARS, DATING WOULD BE IMPOSSIBLE. NO DATING, THEN NO MARRIAGE. SOON THE SPECIES WOULD BE EXTINCT.

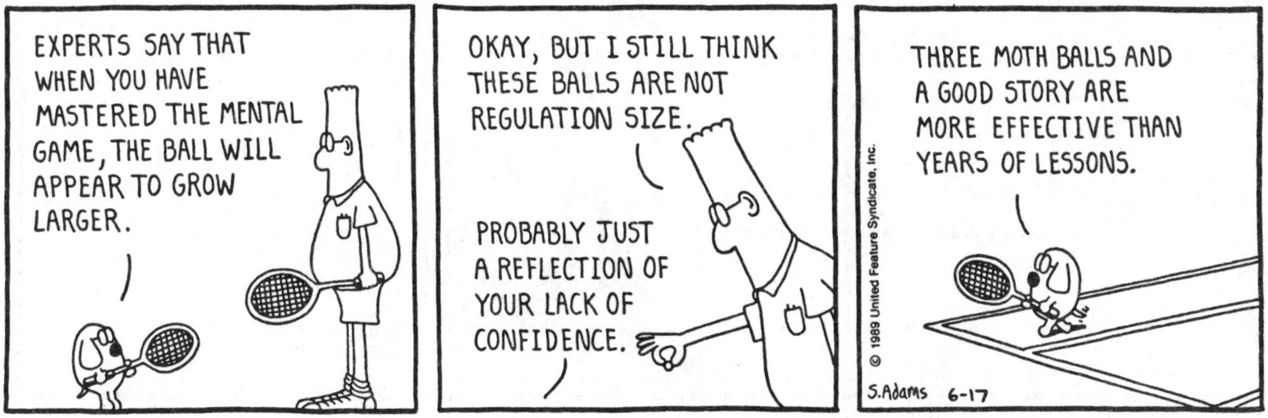
EXPERTS SAY THAT WHEN YOU HAVE MASTERED THE MENTAL GAME, THE BALL WILL APPEAR TO GROW LARGER.
OKAY, BUT I STILL THINK THESE BALLS ARE NOT REGULATION SIZE.
PROBABLY JUST A REFLECTION OF YOUR LACK OF CONFIDENCE.
© 1989 United Feature Syndicate, Inc.
THREE MOTH BALLS AND A GOOD STORY ARE MORE EFFECTIVE THAN YEARS OF LESSONS.
S.Adams 6-17

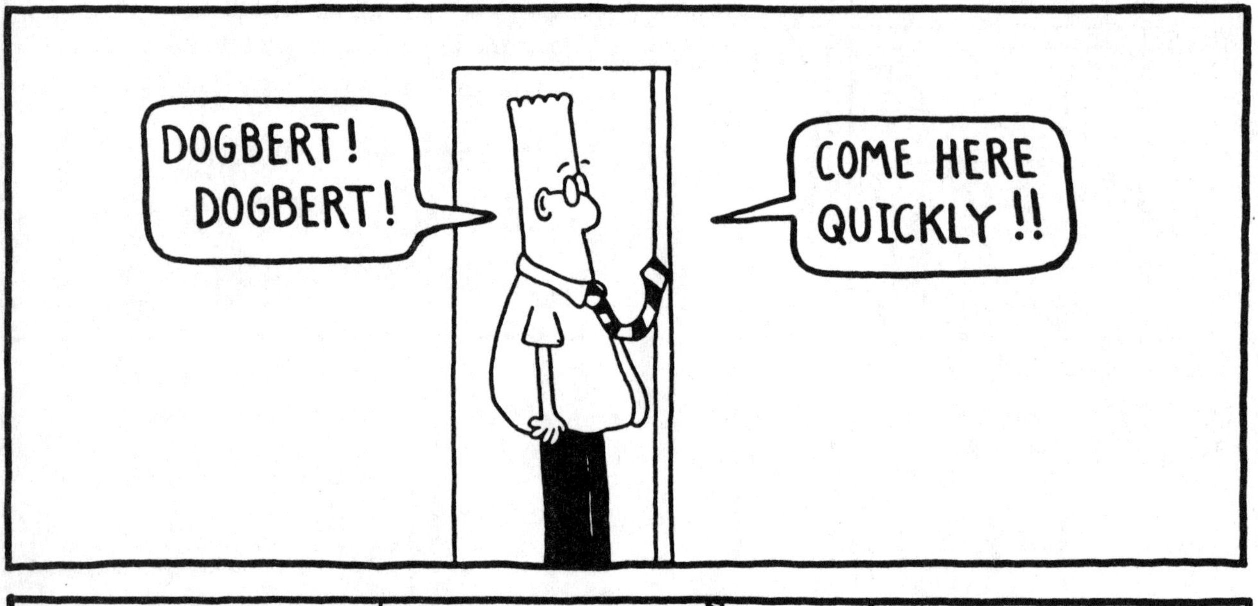
DOGBERT! DOGBERT!
COME HERE QUICKLY !!
MY COMPUTER SIM - ULATION HAS DISCOVERED THE CHEMICAL THAT CAUSES LOVE !

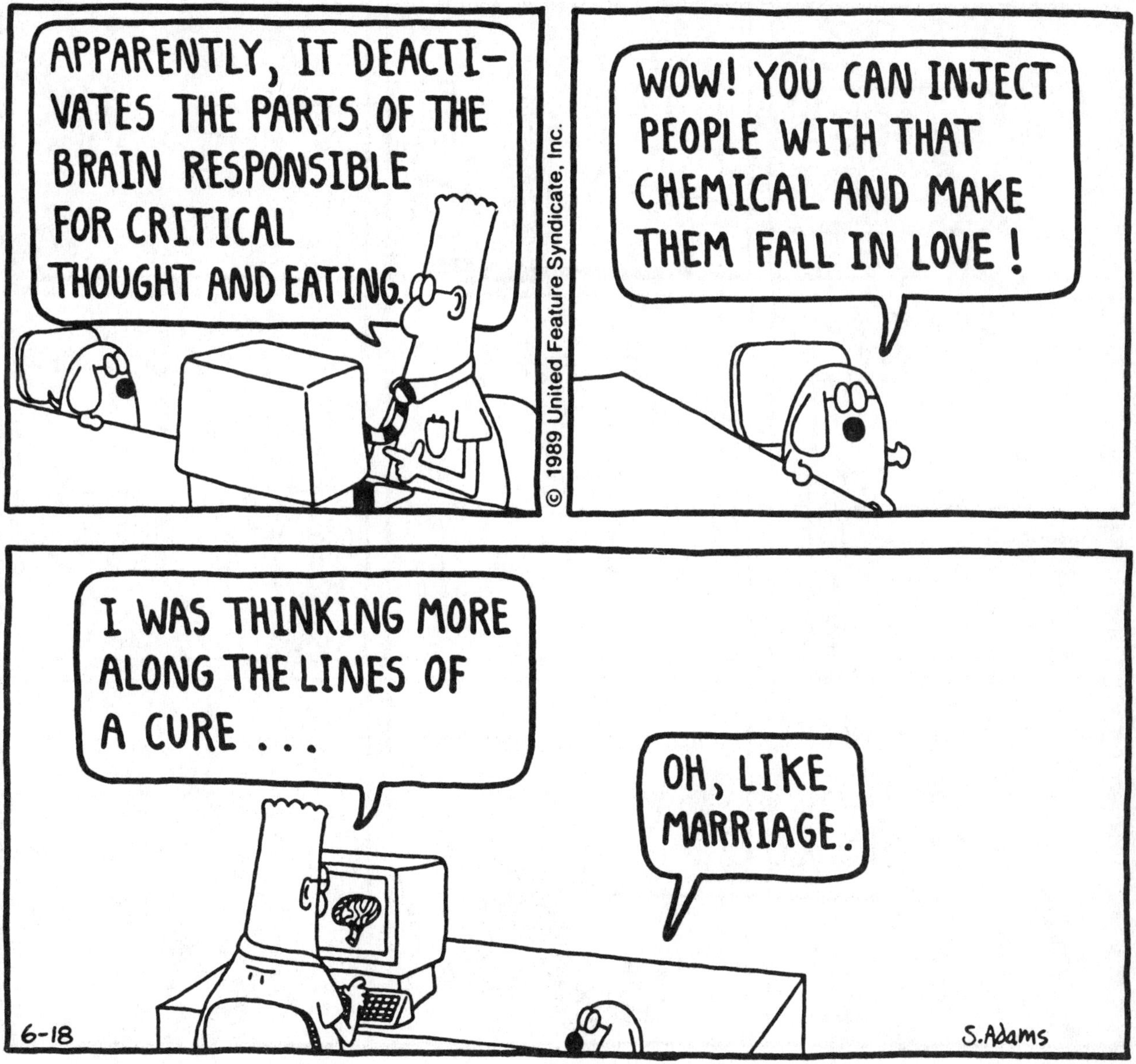
APPARENTLY, IT DEACTIVATES THE PARTS OF THE BRAIN RESPONSIBLE FOR CRITICAL THOUGHT AND EATING.
© 1989 United Feature Syndicate, Inc.
WOW! YOU CAN INJECT PEOPLE WITH THAT CHEMICAL AND MAKE THEM FALL IN LOVE!
I WAS THINKING MORE ALONG THE LINES OF A CURE . . .
OH, LIKE MARRIAGE.
6-18
S. Adams

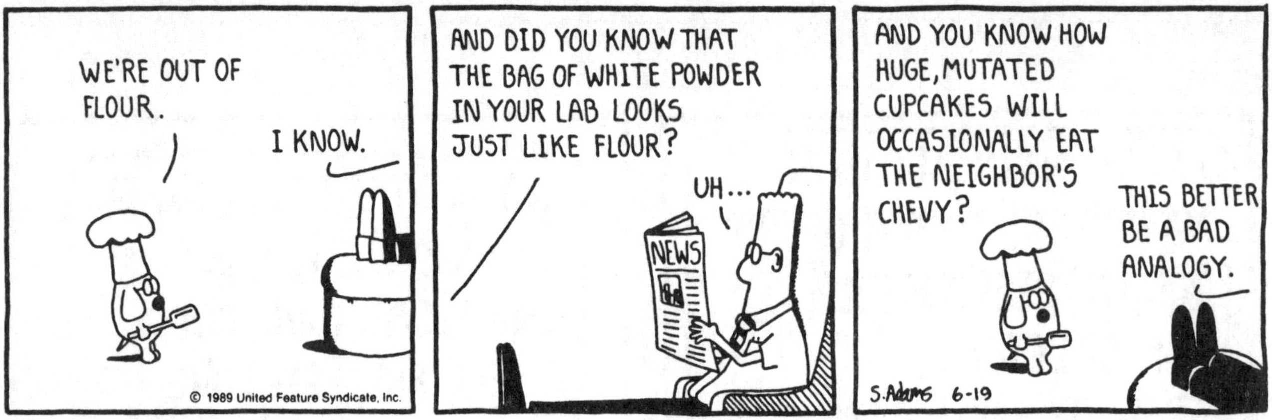
WE'RE OUT OF FLOUR.
I KNOW.
© 1989 United Feature Syndicate, Inc.
AND DID YOU KNOW THAT THE BAG OF WHITE POWDER IN YOUR LAB LOOKS JUST LIKE FLOUR?
UH...
NEWS
AND YOU KNOW HOW HUGE, MUTATED CUPCAKES WILL OCCASIONALLY EAT THE NEIGHBOR'S CHEVY?
THIS BETTER BE A BAD ANALOGY.
S.Adams 6-19

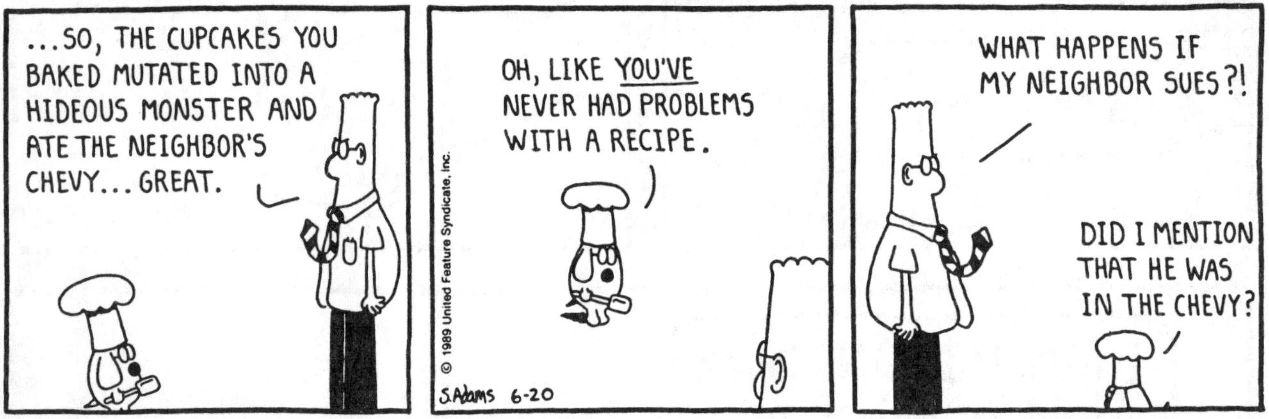
...SO, THE CUPCAKES YOU BAKED MUTATED INTO A HIDEOUS MONSTER AND ATE THE NEIGHBOR'S CHEVY... GREAT.
OH, LIKE YOU'VE NEVER HAD PROBLEMS WITH A RECIPE.
© 1989 United Feature Syndicate, Inc.
S.Adams 6-20
WHAT HAPPENS IF MY NEIGHBOR SUES?!
DID I MENTION THAT HE WAS IN THE CHEVY?

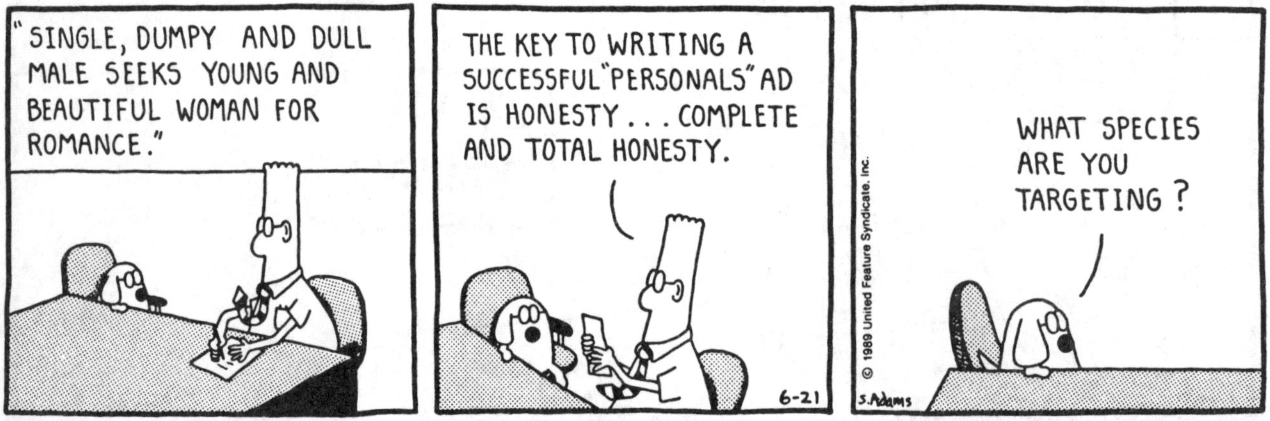
"SINGLE, DUMPY AND DULL MALE SEEKS YOUNG AND BEAUTIFUL WOMAN FOR ROMANCE."
THE KEY TO WRITING A SUCCESSFUL "PERSONALS" AD IS HONESTY . . . COMPLETE AND TOTAL HONESTY.
6-21
WHAT SPECIES ARE YOU TARGETING?
© 1989 United Feature Syndicate, Inc.
S.Adams

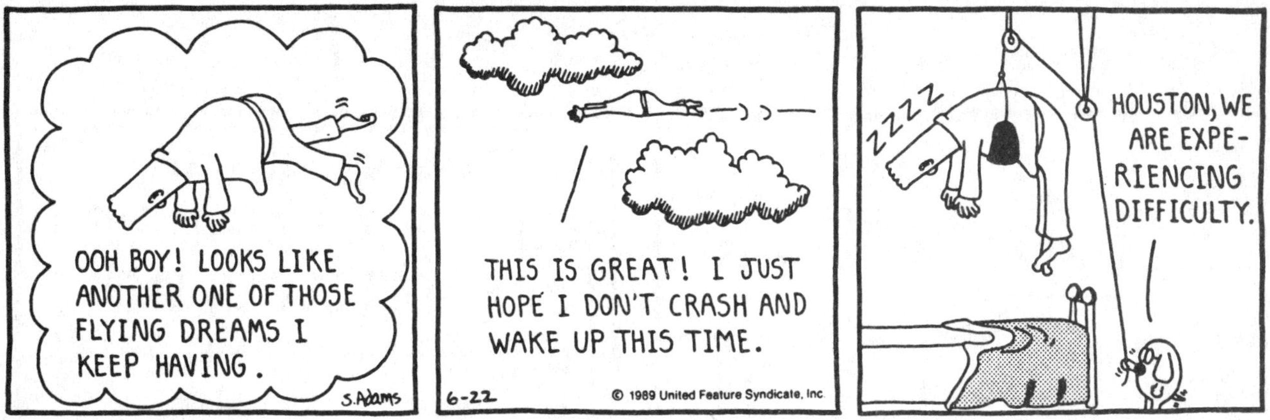
OOH BOY! LOOKS LIKE ANOTHER ONE OF THOSE FLYING DREAMS I KEEP HAVING.
S.Adams
THIS IS GREAT! I JUST HOPE I DON'T CRASH AND WAKE UP THIS TIME.
6-22
© 1989 United Feature Syndicate, Inc.
ZZZZ
HOUSTON, WE ARE EXPE-RIENCING DIFFICULTY.

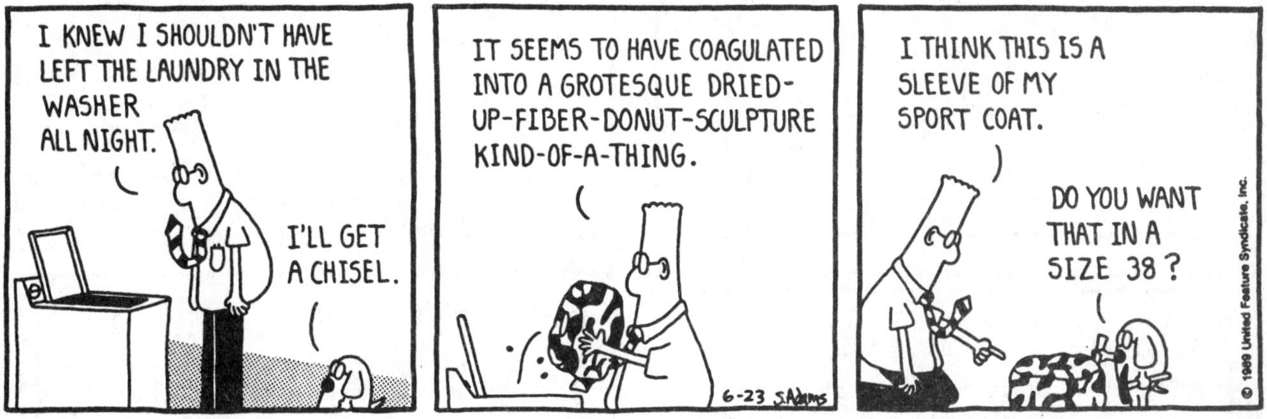
I KNEW I SHOULDN'T HAVE LEFT THE LAUNDRY IN THE WASHER ALL NIGHT.
I'LL GET A CHISEL.
IT SEEMS TO HAVE COAGULATED INTO A GROTESQUE DRIED-UP-FIBER-DONUT-SCULPTURE KIND-OF-A-THING.
6-23 S.Adams
I THINK THIS IS A SLEEVE OF MY SPORT COAT.
DO YOU WANT THAT IN A SIZE 38?
© 1989 United Feature Syndicate, Inc.

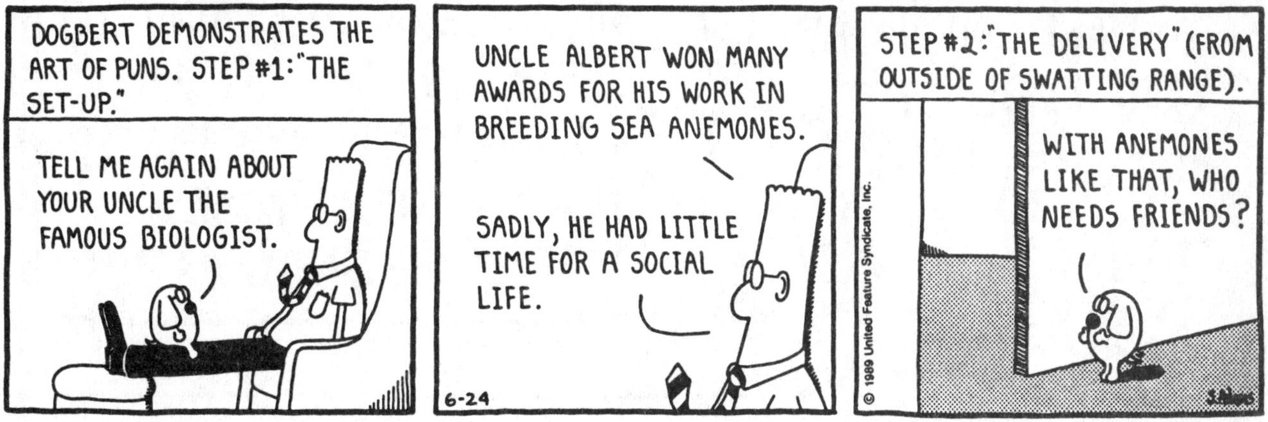
DOGBERT DEMONSTRATES THE ART OF PUNS. STEP #1: "THE SET-UP."
TELL ME AGAIN ABOUT YOUR UNCLE THE FAMOUS BIOLOGIST.
UNCLE ALBERT WON MANY AWARDS FOR HIS WORK IN BREEDING SEA ANEMONES.
SADLY, HE HAD LITTLE TIME FOR A SOCIAL LIFE.
6-24
© 1989 United Feature Syndicate, Inc.
STEP #2: "THE DELIVERY" (FROM OUTSIDE OF SWATTING RANGE).
WITH ANEMONES LIKE THAT, WHO NEEDS FRIENDS?
S.Adams

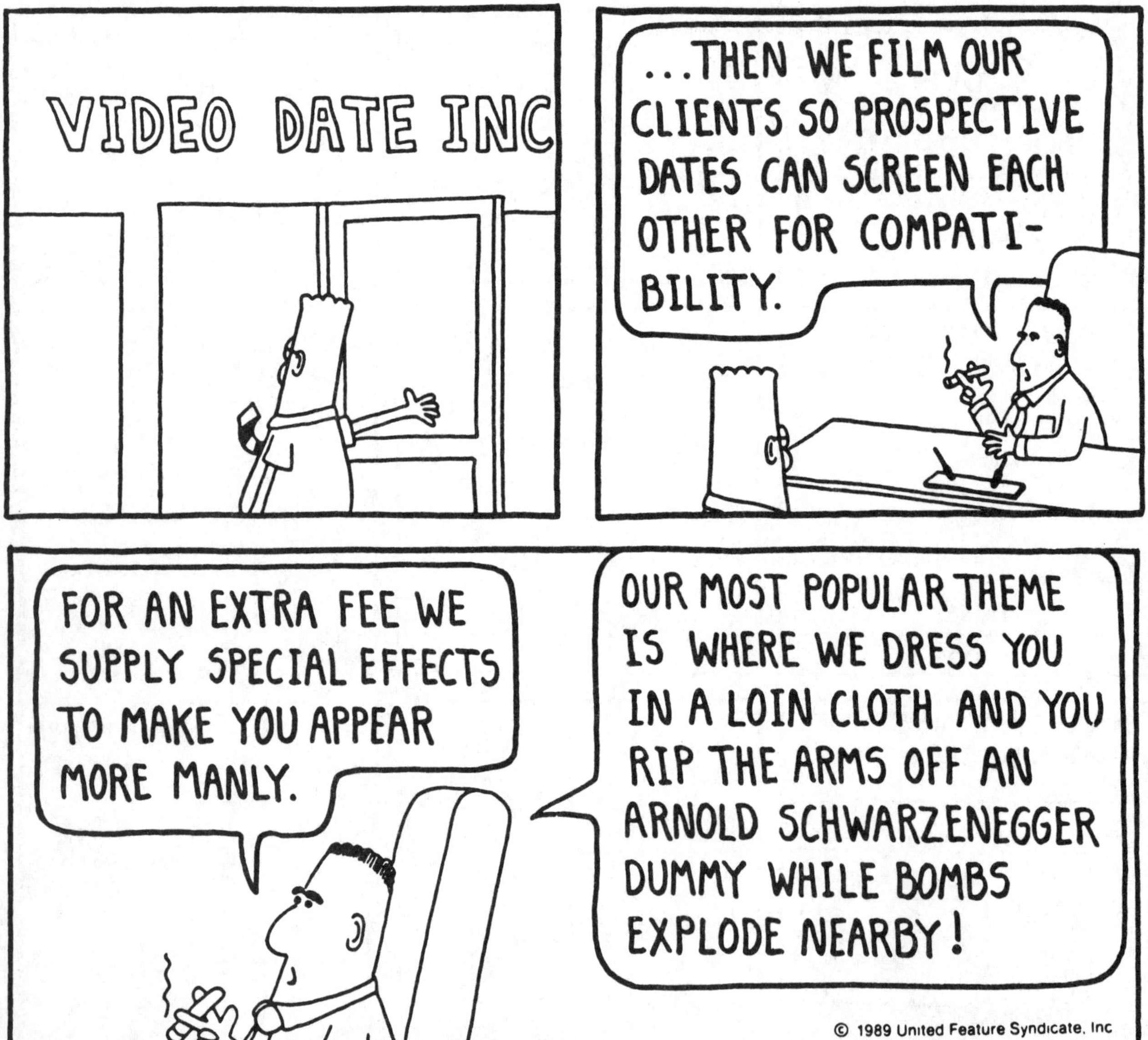
VIDEO DATE INC
...THEN WE FILM OUR CLIENTS SO PROSPECTIVE DATES CAN SCREEN EACH OTHER FOR COMPATI-BILITY.
FOR AN EXTRA FEE WE SUPPLY SPECIAL EFFECTS TO MAKE YOU APPEAR MORE MANLY.
OUR MOST POPULAR THEME IS WHERE WE DRESS YOU IN A LOIN CLOTH AND YOU RIP THE ARMS OFF AN ARNOLD SCHWARZENEGGER DUMMY WHILE BOMBS EXPLODE NEARBY!
© 1989 United Feature Syndicate, Inc

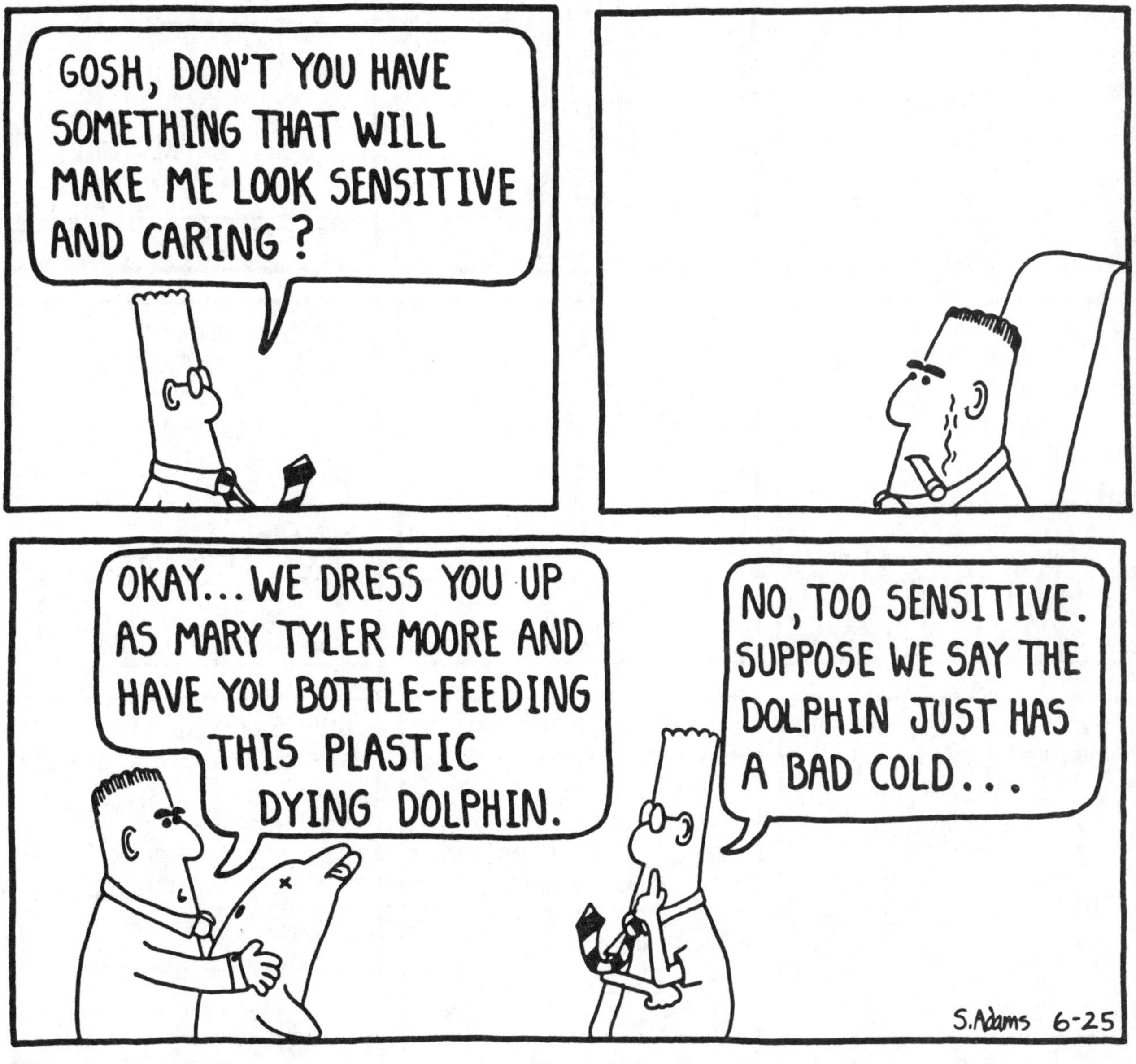
GOSH, DON'T YOU HAVE SOMETHING THAT WILL MAKE ME LOOK SENSITIVE AND CARING?
OKAY... WE DRESS YOU UP AS MARY TYLER MOORE AND HAVE YOU BOTTLE-FEEDING THIS PLASTIC DYING DOLPHIN.
NO, TOO SENSITIVE. SUPPOSE WE SAY THE DOLPHIN JUST HAS A BAD COLD...
S.Adams 6-25

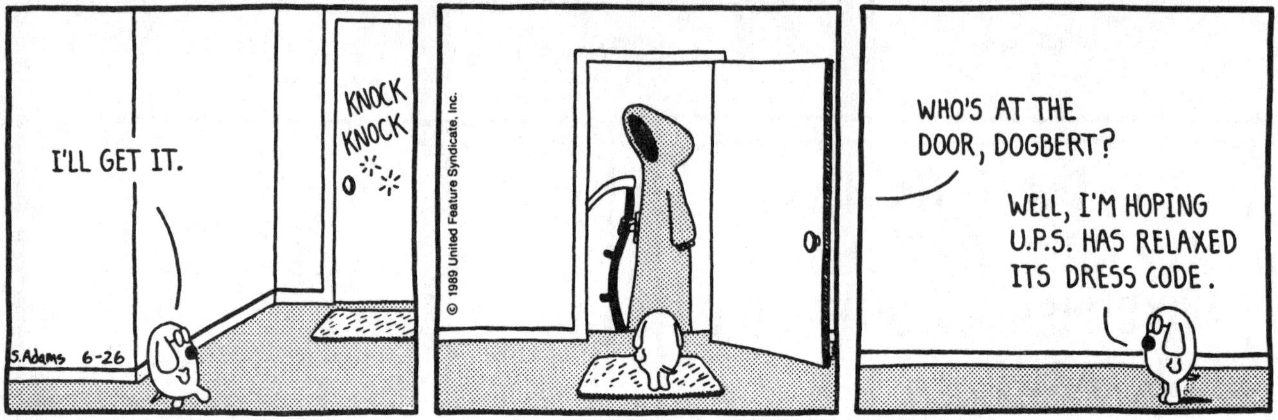
I'LL GET IT.
KNOCK KNOCK
S.Adams 6-26
© 1989 United Feature Syndicate, Inc.
WHO'S AT THE DOOR, DOGBERT?
WELL, I'M HOPING U.P.S. HAS RELAXED ITS DRESS CODE.

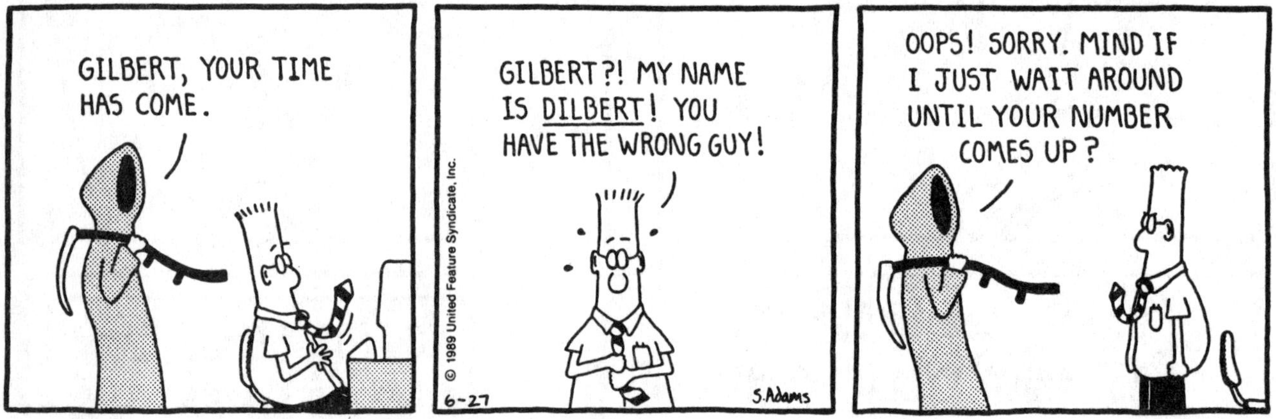
GILBERT, YOUR TIME HAS COME.
GILBERT?! MY NAME IS DILBERT! YOU HAVE THE WRONG GUY!
© 1989 United Feature Syndicate, Inc.
6-27
S.Adams
OOPS! SORRY. MIND IF I JUST WAIT AROUND UNTIL YOUR NUMBER COMES UP?

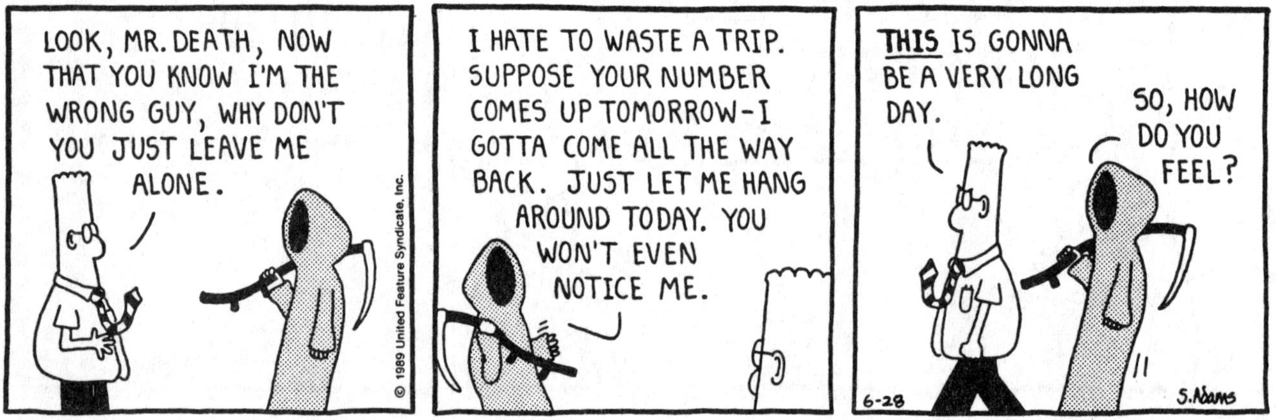
LOOK, MR. DEATH, NOW THAT YOU KNOW I'M THE WRONG GUY, WHY DON'T YOU JUST LEAVE ME ALONE.
© 1989 United Feature Syndicate, Inc.
I HATE TO WASTE A TRIP. SUPPOSE YOUR NUMBER COMES UP TOMORROW-I GOTTA COME ALL THE WAY BACK. JUST LET ME HANG AROUND TODAY. YOU WON'T EVEN NOTICE ME.
THIS IS GONNA BE A VERY LONG DAY.
SO, HOW DO YOU FEEL?
6-28
S.Adams

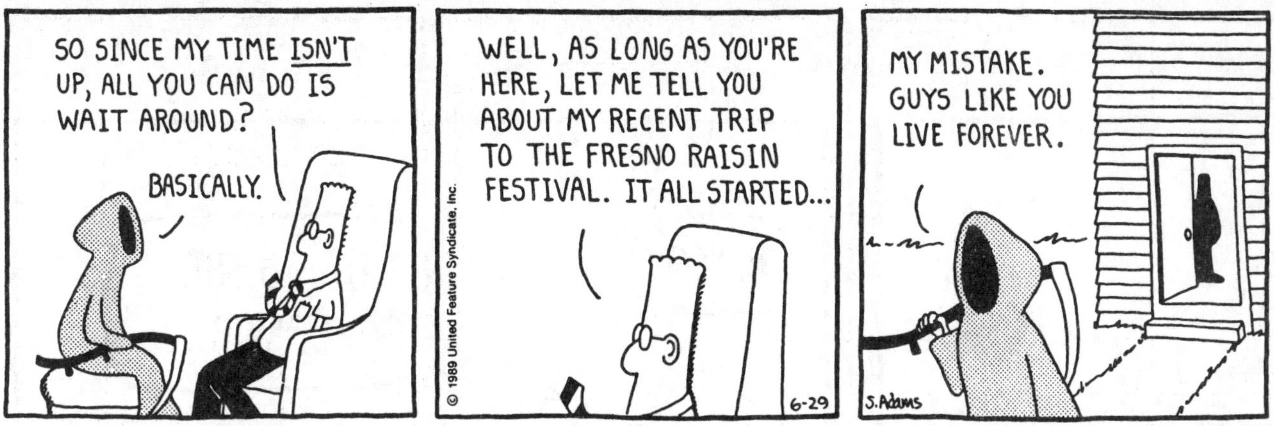
SO SINCE MY TIME ISN'T UP, ALL YOU CAN DO IS WAIT AROUND?
BASICALLY.
WELL, AS LONG AS YOU'RE HERE, LET ME TELL YOU ABOUT MY RECENT TRIP TO THE FRESNO RAISIN FESTIVAL. IT ALL STARTED...
© 1989 United Feature Syndicate, Inc.
6-29
MY MISTAKE. GUYS LIKE YOU LIVE FOREVER.
S. Adams

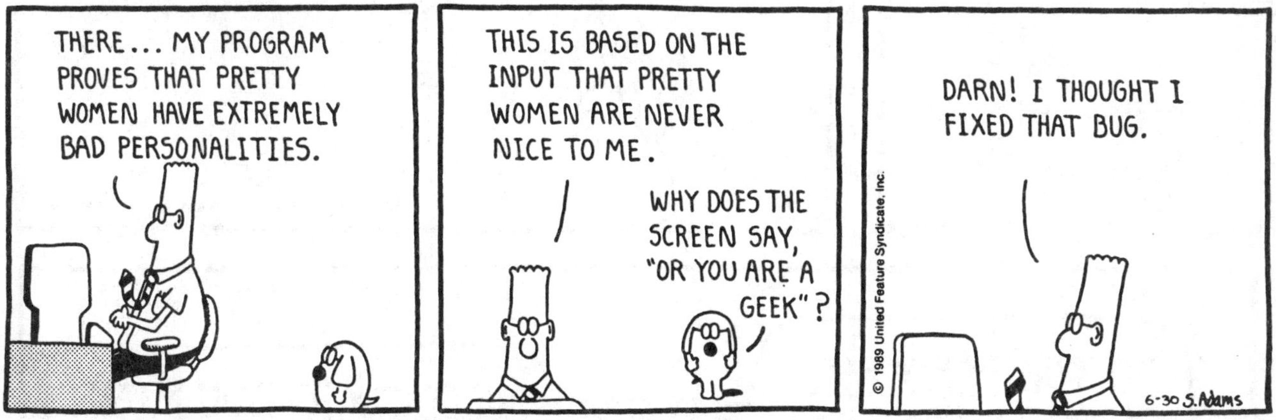
THERE... MY PROGRAM PROVES THAT PRETTY WOMEN HAVE EXTREMELY BAD PERSONALITIES.
THIS IS BASED ON THE INPUT THAT PRETTY WOMEN ARE NEVER NICE TO ME.
WHY DOES THE SCREEN SAY, "OR YOU ARE A GEEK"?
DARN! I THOUGHT I FIXED THAT BUG.
© 1989 United Feature Syndicate, Inc.
6-30 S. Adams

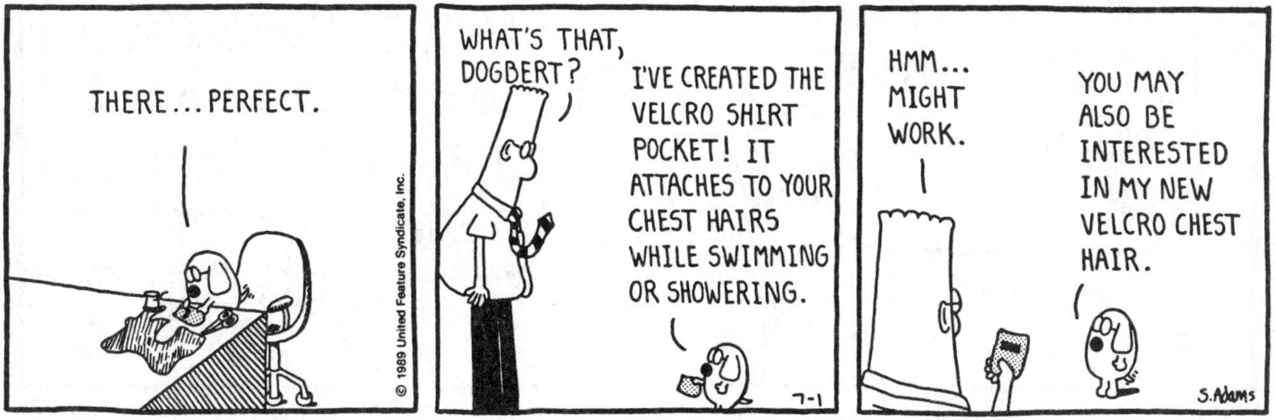
THERE... PERFECT.
© 1989 United Feature Syndicate, Inc.
WHAT'S THAT, DOGBERT?
I'VE CREATED THE VELCRO SHIRT POCKET! IT ATTACHES TO YOUR CHEST HAIRS WHILE SWIMMING OR SHOWERING.
7-1
HMM... MIGHT WORK.
YOU MAY ALSO BE INTERESTED IN MY NEW VELCRO CHEST HAIR.
S. Adams

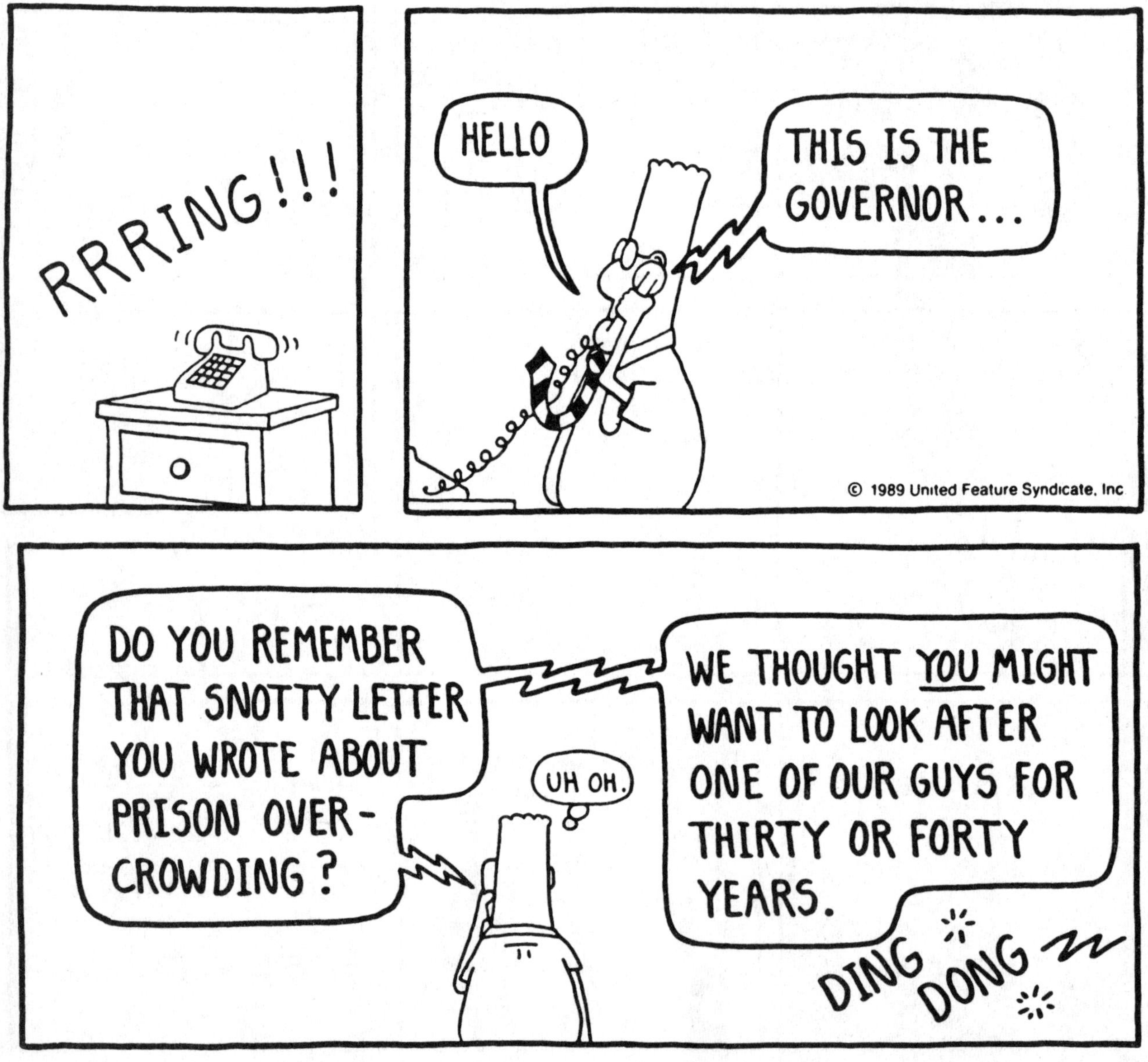
RRRING!!!
HELLO
THIS IS THE GOVERNOR...
© 1989 United Feature Syndicate, Inc
DO YOU REMEMBER THAT SNOTTY LETTER YOU WROTE ABOUT PRISON OVER-CROWDING?
UH OH.
WE THOUGHT YOU MIGHT WANT TO LOOK AFTER ONE OF OUR GUYS FOR THIRTY OR FORTY YEARS.
DING DONG

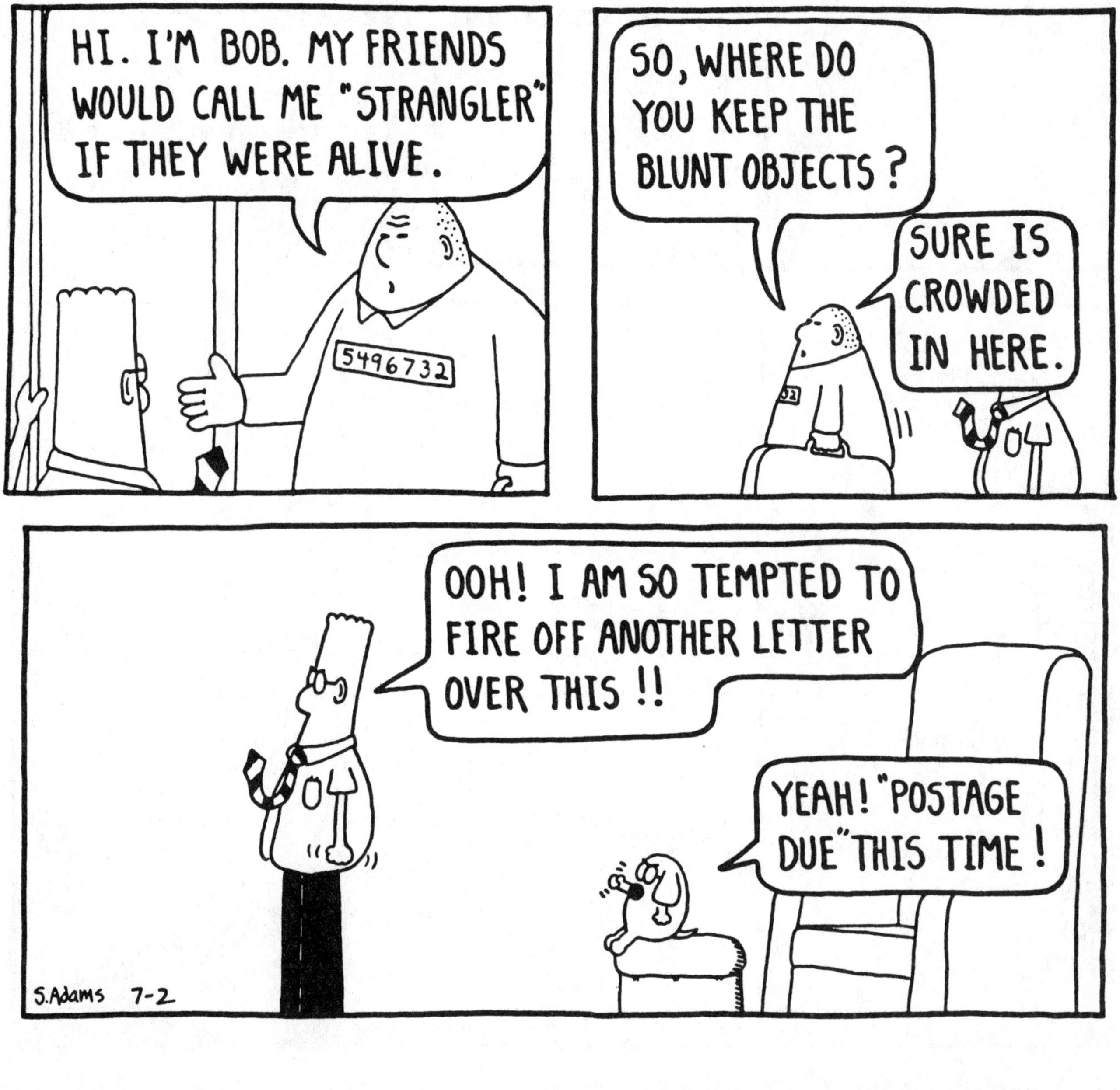
HI. I'M BOB. MY FRIENDS WOULD CALL ME "STRANGLER" IF THEY WERE ALIVE.
5496732
SO, WHERE DO YOU KEEP THE BLUNT OBJECTS?
SURE IS CROWDED IN HERE.
OOH! I AM SO TEMPTED TO FIRE OFF ANOTHER LETTER OVER THIS!!
YEAH! "POSTAGE DUE" THIS TIME!
S.Adams 7-2

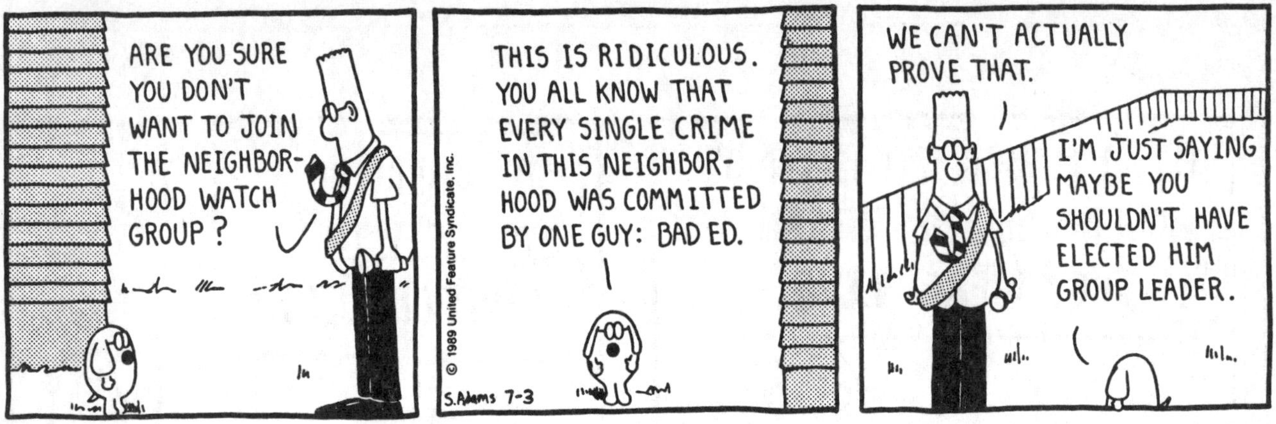
ARE YOU SURE YOU DON'T WANT TO JOIN THE NEIGHBOR-HOOD WATCH GROUP?
THIS IS RIDICULOUS. YOU ALL KNOW THAT EVERY SINGLE CRIME IN THIS NEIGHBOR-HOOD WAS COMMITTED BY ONE GUY: BAD ED.
© 1989 United Feature Syndicate, Inc.
S.Adams 7-3
WE CAN'T ACTUALLY PROVE THAT.
I'M JUST SAYING MAYBE YOU SHOULDN'T HAVE ELECTED HIM GROUP LEADER.

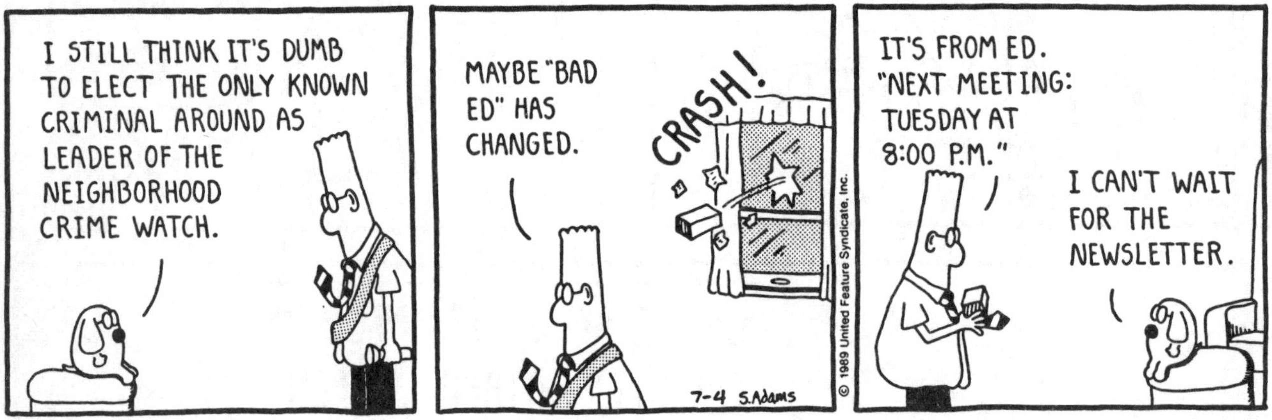
I STILL THINK IT'S DUMB TO ELECT THE ONLY KNOWN CRIMINAL AROUND AS LEADER OF THE NEIGHBORHOOD CRIME WATCH.
MAYBE "BAD ED" HAS CHANGED.
CRASH!
7-4 S.Adams
© 1989 United Feature Syndicate, Inc.
IT'S FROM ED. "NEXT MEETING: TUESDAY AT 8:00 P.M."
I CAN'T WAIT FOR THE NEWSLETTER.

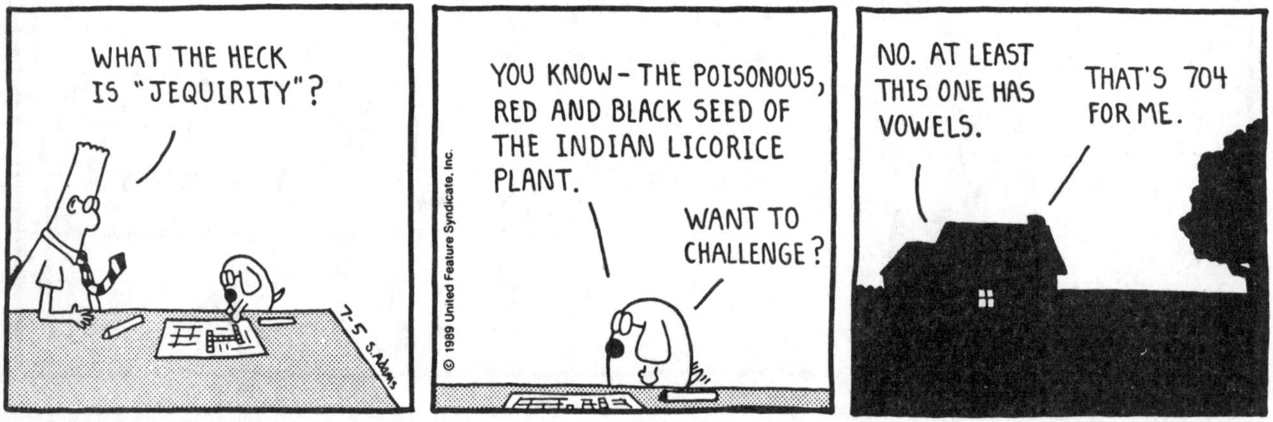
WHAT THE HECK IS "JEQUIRITY"?
7-5 S.Adams
© 1989 United Feature Syndicate, Inc.
YOU KNOW - THE POISONOUS, RED AND BLACK SEED OF THE INDIAN LICORICE PLANT.
WANT TO CHALLENGE?
NO. AT LEAST THIS ONE HAS VOWELS.
THAT'S 704 FOR ME.

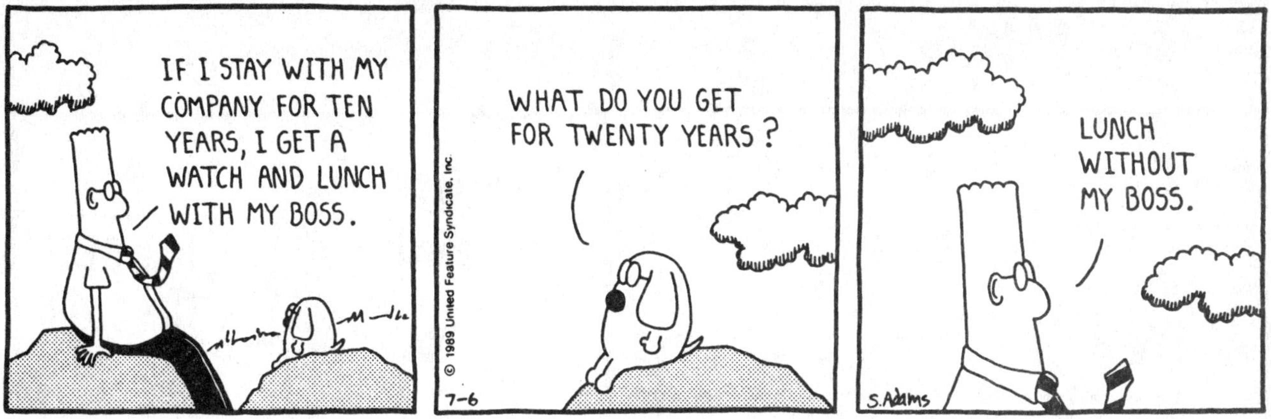
IF I STAY WITH MY COMPANY FOR TEN YEARS, I GET A WATCH AND LUNCH WITH MY BOSS.
© 1989 United Feature Syndicate, Inc.
WHAT DO YOU GET FOR TWENTY YEARS ?
7-6
LUNCH WITHOUT MY BOSS.
S.Adams

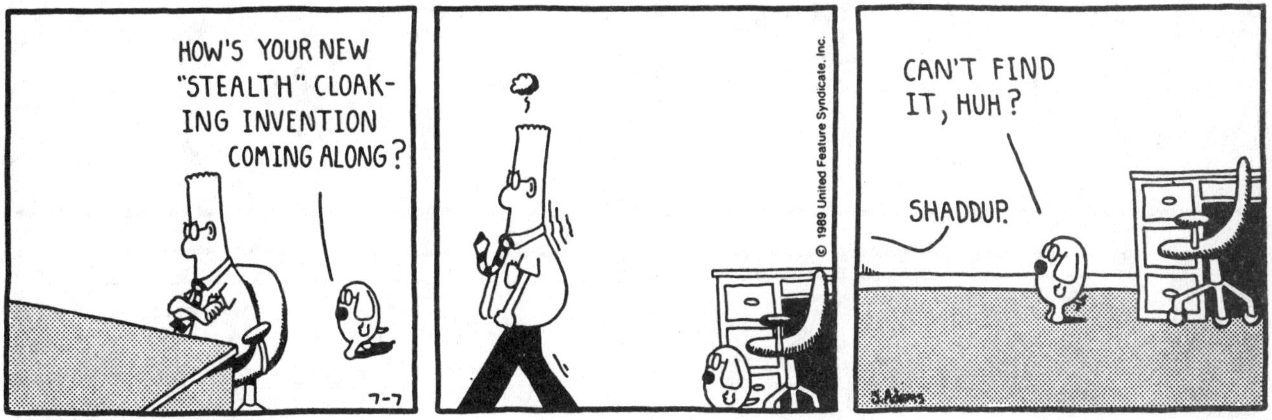
HOW'S YOUR NEW "STEALTH" CLOAKING INVENTION COMING ALONG ?
7-7
© 1989 United Feature Syndicate, Inc.
CAN'T FIND IT, HUH ?
SHADDUP.
S.Adams

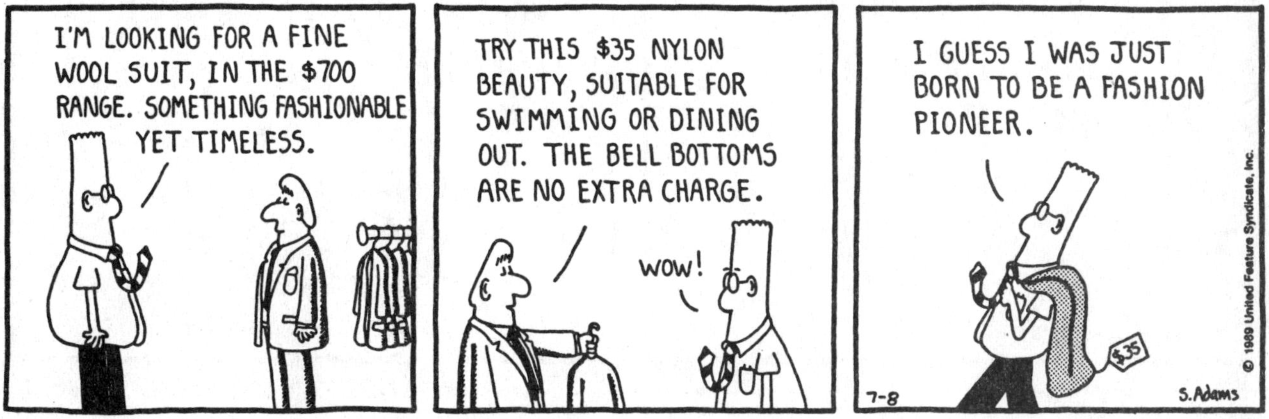
I'M LOOKING FOR A FINE WOOL SUIT, IN THE $700 RANGE. SOMETHING FASHIONABLE YET TIMELESS.
TRY THIS $35 NYLON BEAUTY, SUITABLE FOR SWIMMING OR DINING OUT. THE BELL BOTTOMS ARE NO EXTRA CHARGE.
WOW!
7-8
I GUESS I WAS JUST BORN TO BE A FASHION PIONEER.
$35
© 1989 United Feature Syndicate, Inc.
S.Adams

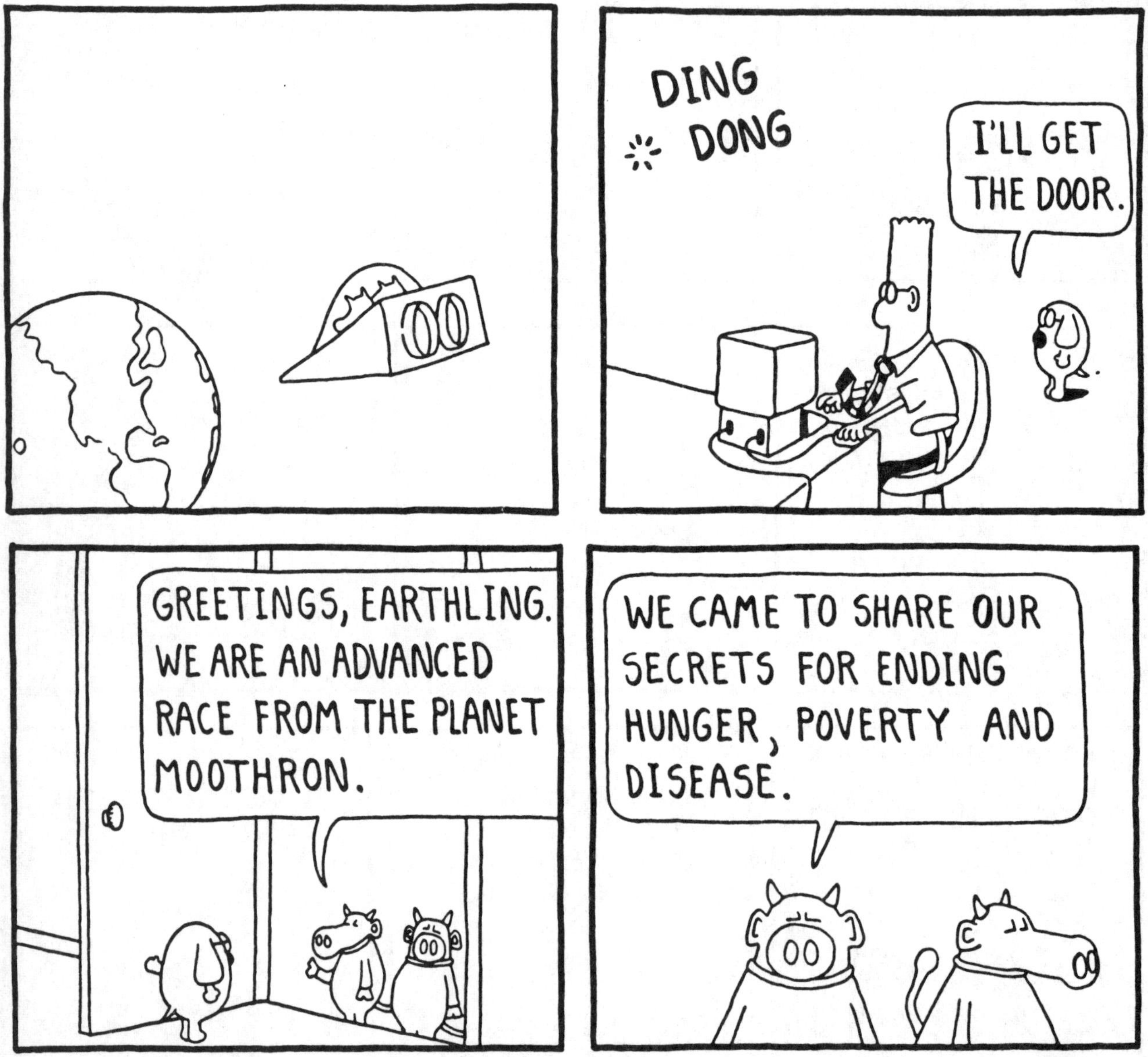
DING DONG
I'LL GET THE DOOR.
GREETINGS, EARTHLING. WE ARE AN ADVANCED RACE FROM THE PLANET MOOTHRON.
WE CAME TO SHARE OUR SECRETS FOR ENDING HUNGER, POVERTY AND DISEASE.

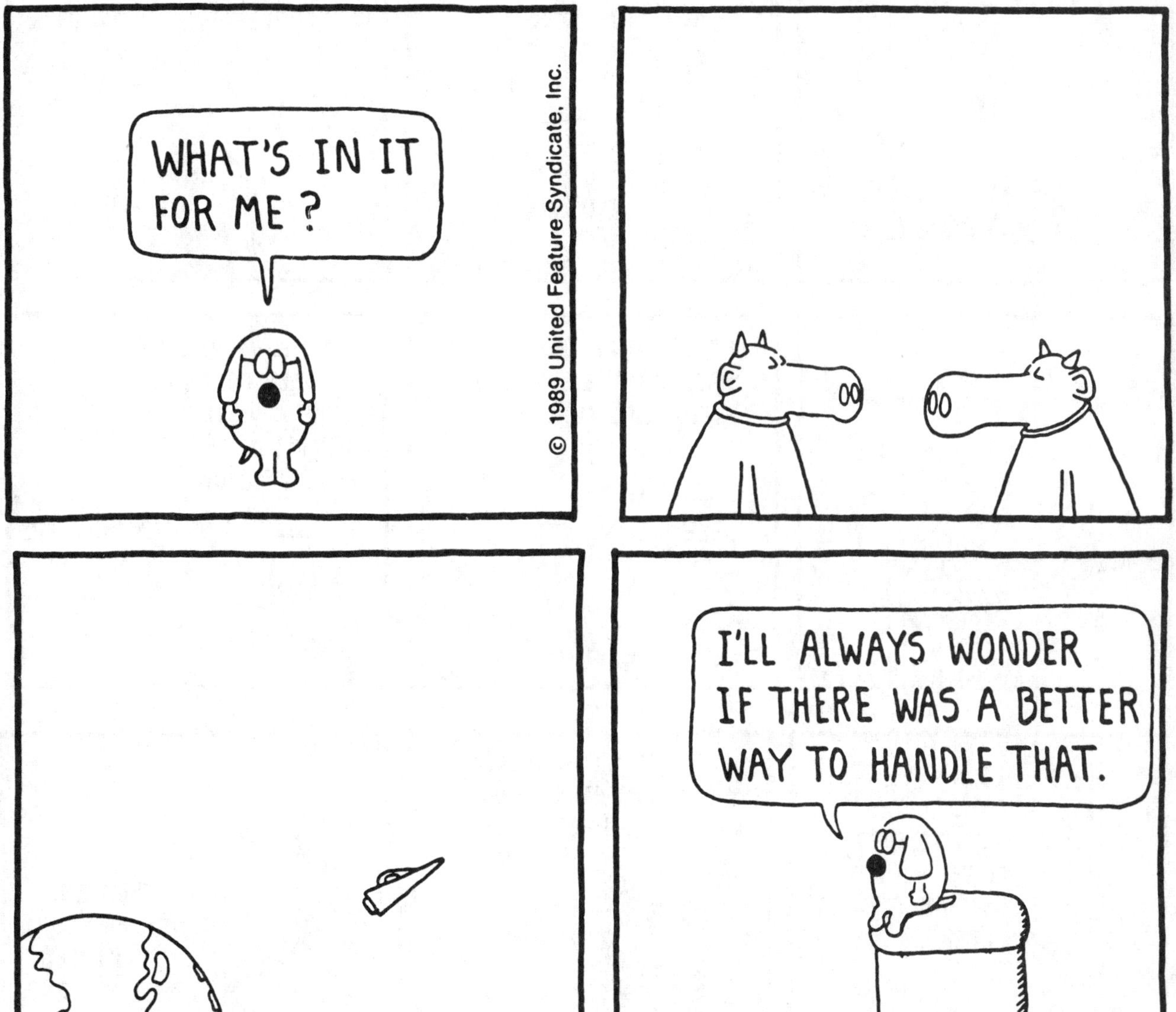
WHAT'S IN IT FOR ME ?
© 1989 United Feature Syndicate, Inc.
I'LL ALWAYS WONDER IF THERE WAS A BETTER WAY TO HANDLE THAT.
S. Adams 7-9

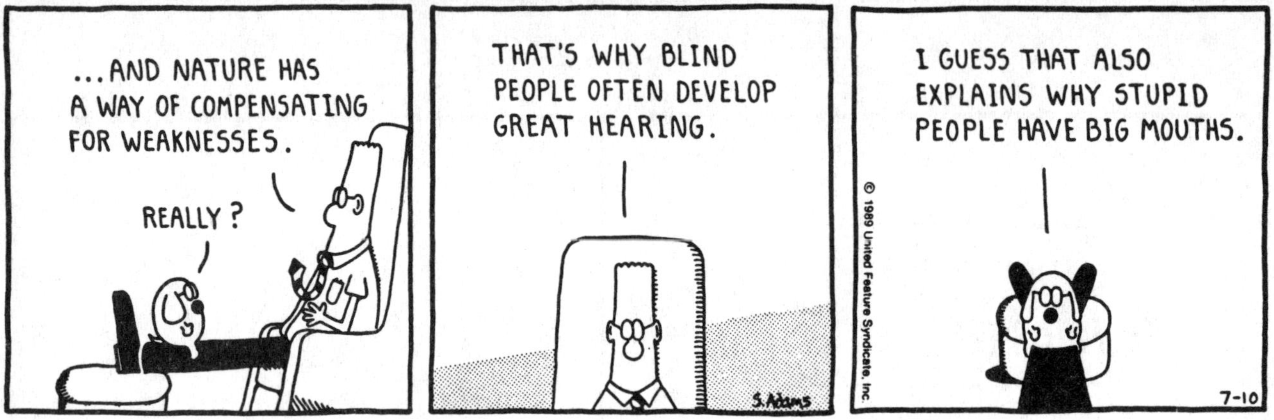
...AND NATURE HAS A WAY OF COMPENSATING FOR WEAKNESSES.
REALLY?
THAT'S WHY BLIND PEOPLE OFTEN DEVELOP GREAT HEARING.
S. Adams
© 1989 United Feature Syndicate, Inc.
I GUESS THAT ALSO EXPLAINS WHY STUPID PEOPLE HAVE BIG MOUTHS.
7-10

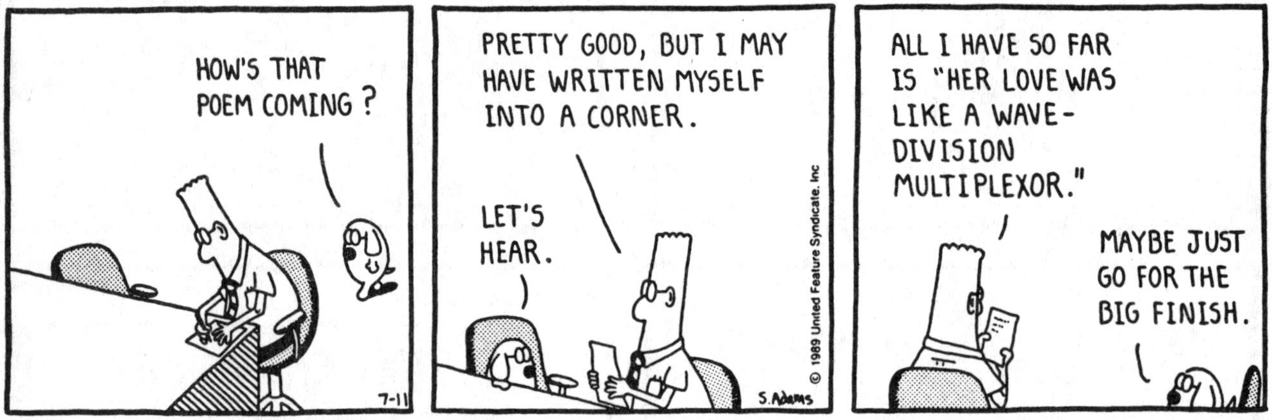
HOW'S THAT POEM COMING?
7-11
PRETTY GOOD, BUT I MAY HAVE WRITTEN MYSELF INTO A CORNER.
LET'S HEAR.
© 1989 United Feature Syndicate, Inc
S. Adams
ALL I HAVE SO FAR IS "HER LOVE WAS LIKE A WAVE-DIVISION MULTIPLEXOR."
MAYBE JUST GO FOR THE BIG FINISH.

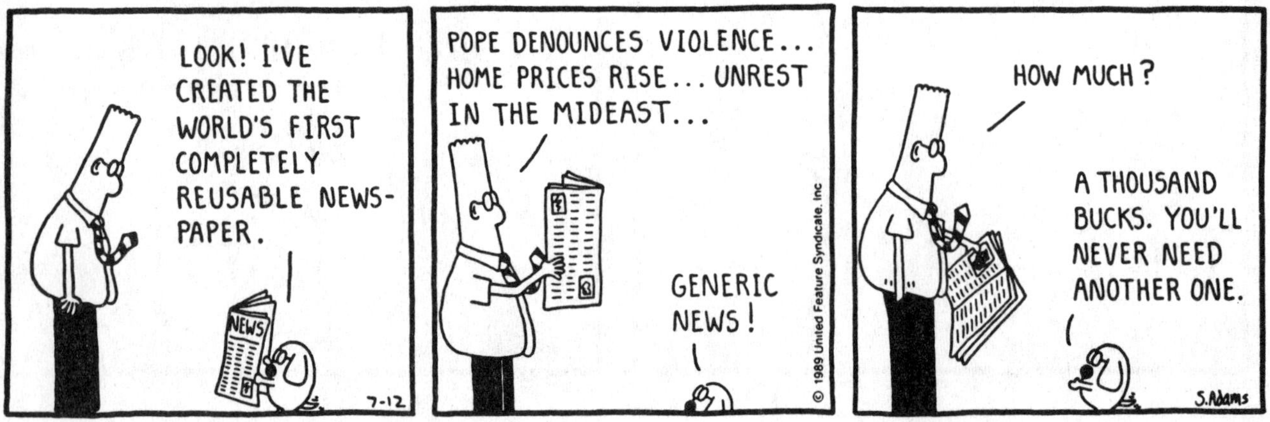
LOOK! I'VE CREATED THE WORLD'S FIRST COMPLETELY REUSABLE NEWS-PAPER.
NEWS
7-12
POPE DENOUNCES VIOLENCE... HOME PRICES RISE... UNREST IN THE MIDEAST...
GENERIC NEWS!
© 1989 United Feature Syndicate, Inc
HOW MUCH?
A THOUSAND BUCKS. YOU'LL NEVER NEED ANOTHER ONE.
S. Adams

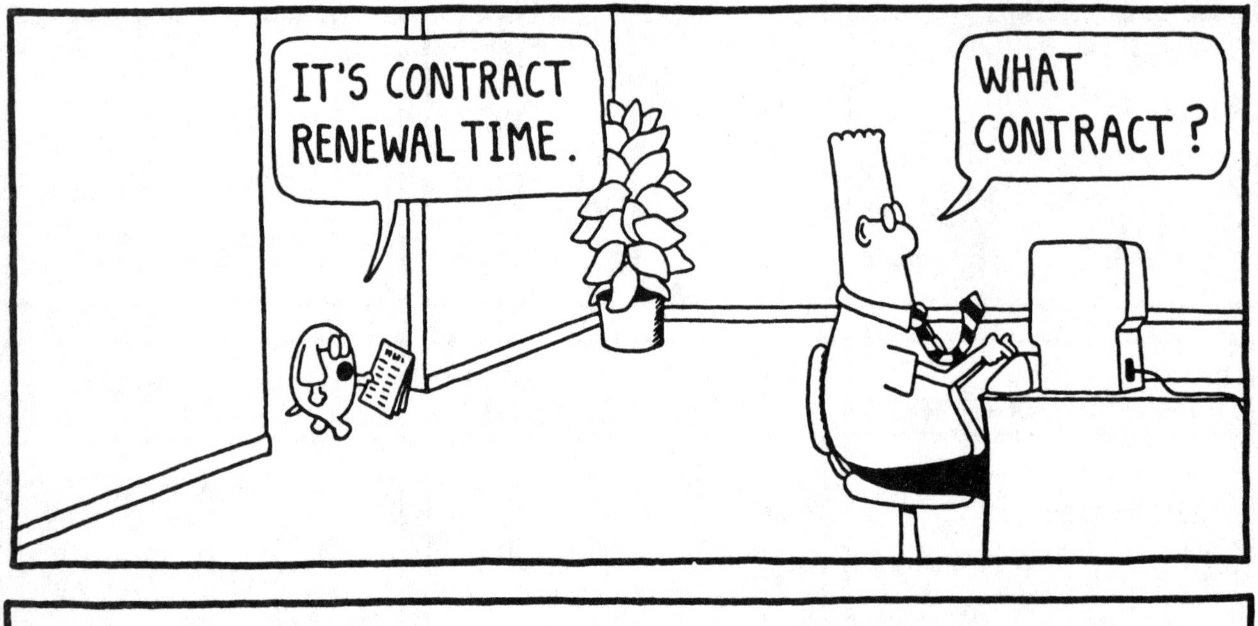
IT'S CONTRACT RENEWAL TIME.
WHAT CONTRACT?
THE OWNER/PET CONTRACT; OURS EXPIRES AT MIDNIGHT.
GOSH. I DON'T EVEN REMEMBER SIGNING THE ORIGINAL ONE.

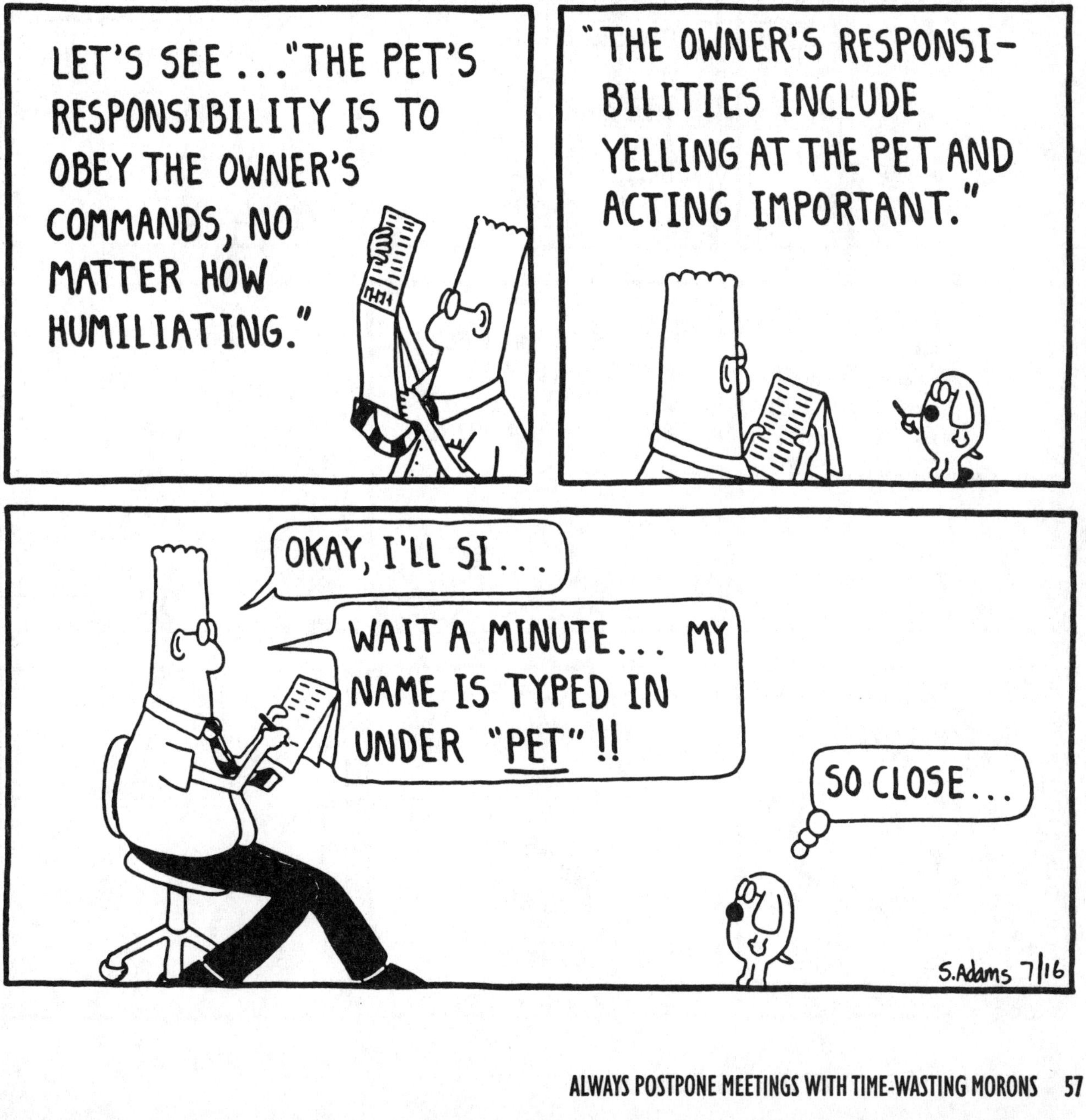
LET'S SEE ... "THE PET'S RESPONSIBILITY IS TO OBEY THE OWNER'S COMMANDS, NO MATTER HOW HUMILIATING."
"THE OWNER'S RESPONSIBILITIES INCLUDE YELLING AT THE PET AND ACTING IMPORTANT."
OKAY, I'LL SI...
WAIT A MINUTE... MY NAME IS TYPED IN UNDER "PET" !!
SO CLOSE...
S.Adams 7/16

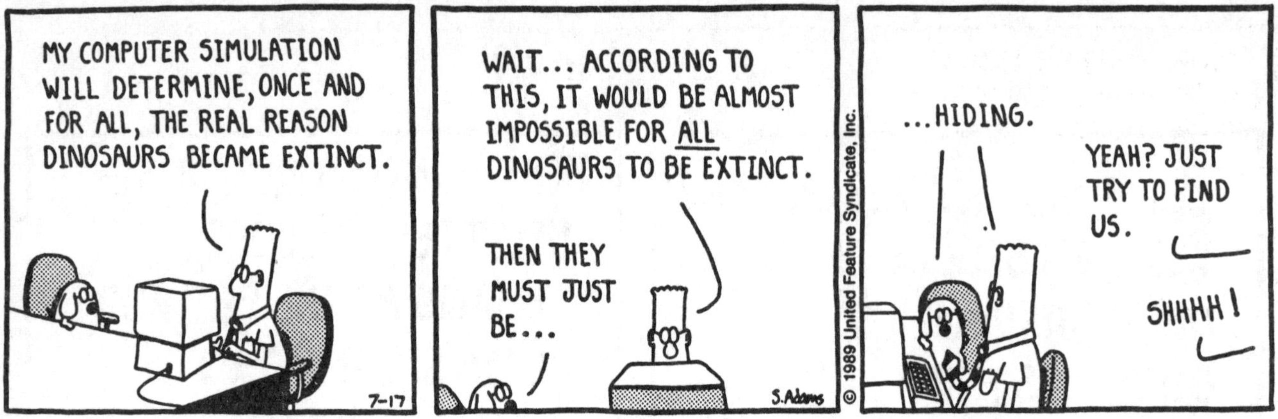
MY COMPUTER SIMULATION WILL DETERMINE, ONCE AND FOR ALL, THE REAL REASON DINOSAURS BECAME EXTINCT.
7-17
WAIT... ACCORDING TO THIS, IT WOULD BE ALMOST IMPOSSIBLE FOR ALL DINOSAURS TO BE EXTINCT.
THEN THEY MUST JUST BE...
S.Adams
© 1989 United Feature Syndicate, Inc.
...HIDING.
YEAH? JUST TRY TO FIND US.
SHHHH!

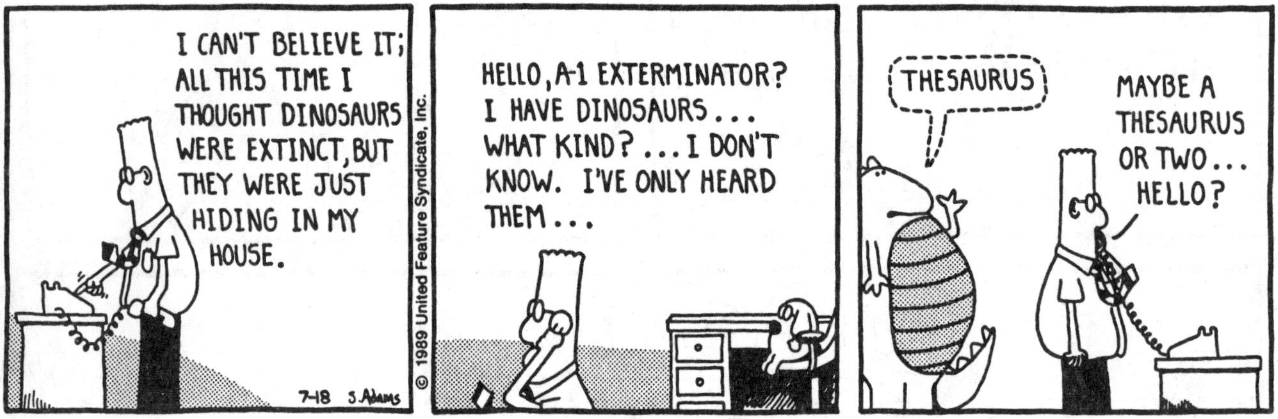
I CAN'T BELIEVE IT; ALL THIS TIME I THOUGHT DINOSAURS WERE EXTINCT, BUT THEY WERE JUST HIDING IN MY HOUSE.
7-18 S.Adams
© 1989 United Feature Syndicate, Inc.
HELLO, A-1 EXTERMINATOR? I HAVE DINOSAURS... WHAT KIND? ...I DON'T KNOW. I'VE ONLY HEARD THEM...
THESAURUS
MAYBE A THESAURUS OR TWO... HELLO?

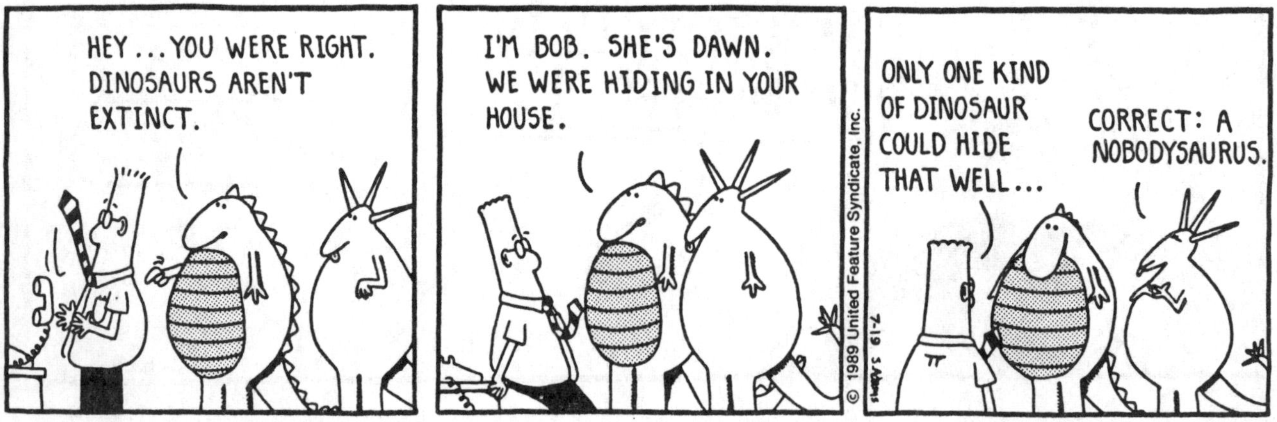
HEY... YOU WERE RIGHT. DINOSAURS AREN'T EXTINCT.
I'M BOB. SHE'S DAWN. WE WERE HIDING IN YOUR HOUSE.
© 1989 United Feature Syndicate, Inc.
7-19 S.Adams
ONLY ONE KIND OF DINOSAUR COULD HIDE THAT WELL...
CORRECT: A NOBODYSAURUS.

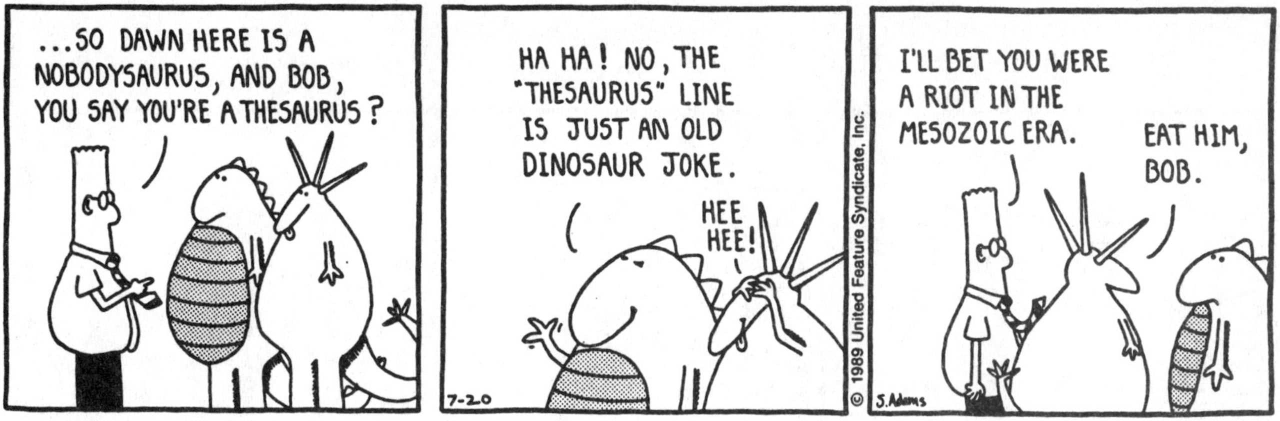
...SO DAWN HERE IS A NOBODYSAURUS, AND BOB, YOU SAY YOU'RE A THESAURUS?
HA HA! NO, THE "THESAURUS" LINE IS JUST AN OLD DINOSAUR JOKE.
HEE HEE!
7-20
© 1989 United Feature Syndicate, Inc.
I'LL BET YOU WERE A RIOT IN THE MESOZOIC ERA.
EAT HIM, BOB.
S. Adams

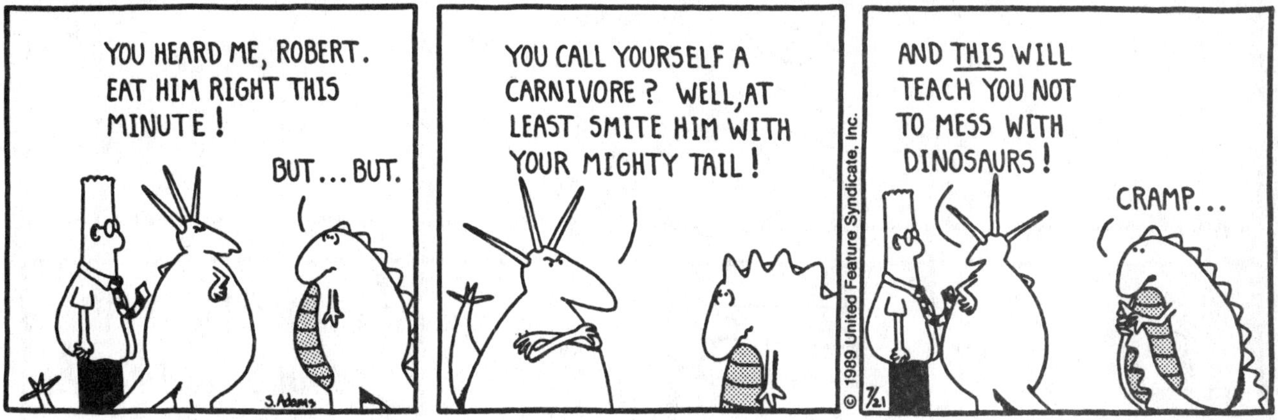
YOU HEARD ME, ROBERT. EAT HIM RIGHT THIS MINUTE!
BUT... BUT.
S. Adams
YOU CALL YOURSELF A CARNIVORE? WELL, AT LEAST SMITE HIM WITH YOUR MIGHTY TAIL!
© 1989 United Feature Syndicate, Inc.
7/21
AND THIS WILL TEACH YOU NOT TO MESS WITH DINOSAURS!
CRAMP...

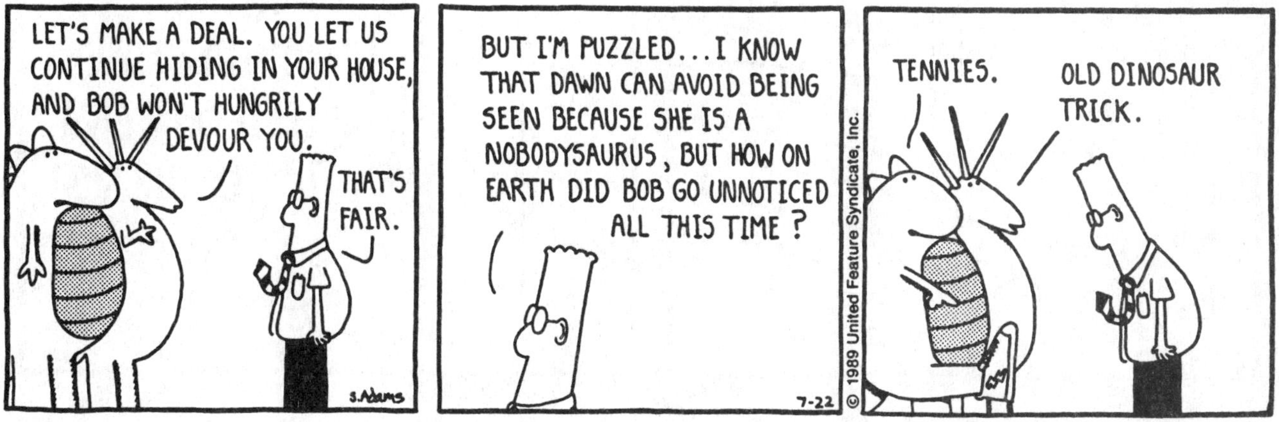
LET'S MAKE A DEAL. YOU LET US CONTINUE HIDING IN YOUR HOUSE, AND BOB WON'T HUNGRILY DEVOUR YOU.
THAT'S FAIR.
S. Adams
BUT I'M PUZZLED... I KNOW THAT DAWN CAN AVOID BEING SEEN BECAUSE SHE IS A NOBODYSAURUS, BUT HOW ON EARTH DID BOB GO UNNOTICED ALL THIS TIME?
7-22
© 1989 United Feature Syndicate, Inc.
TENNIES.
OLD DINOSAUR TRICK.

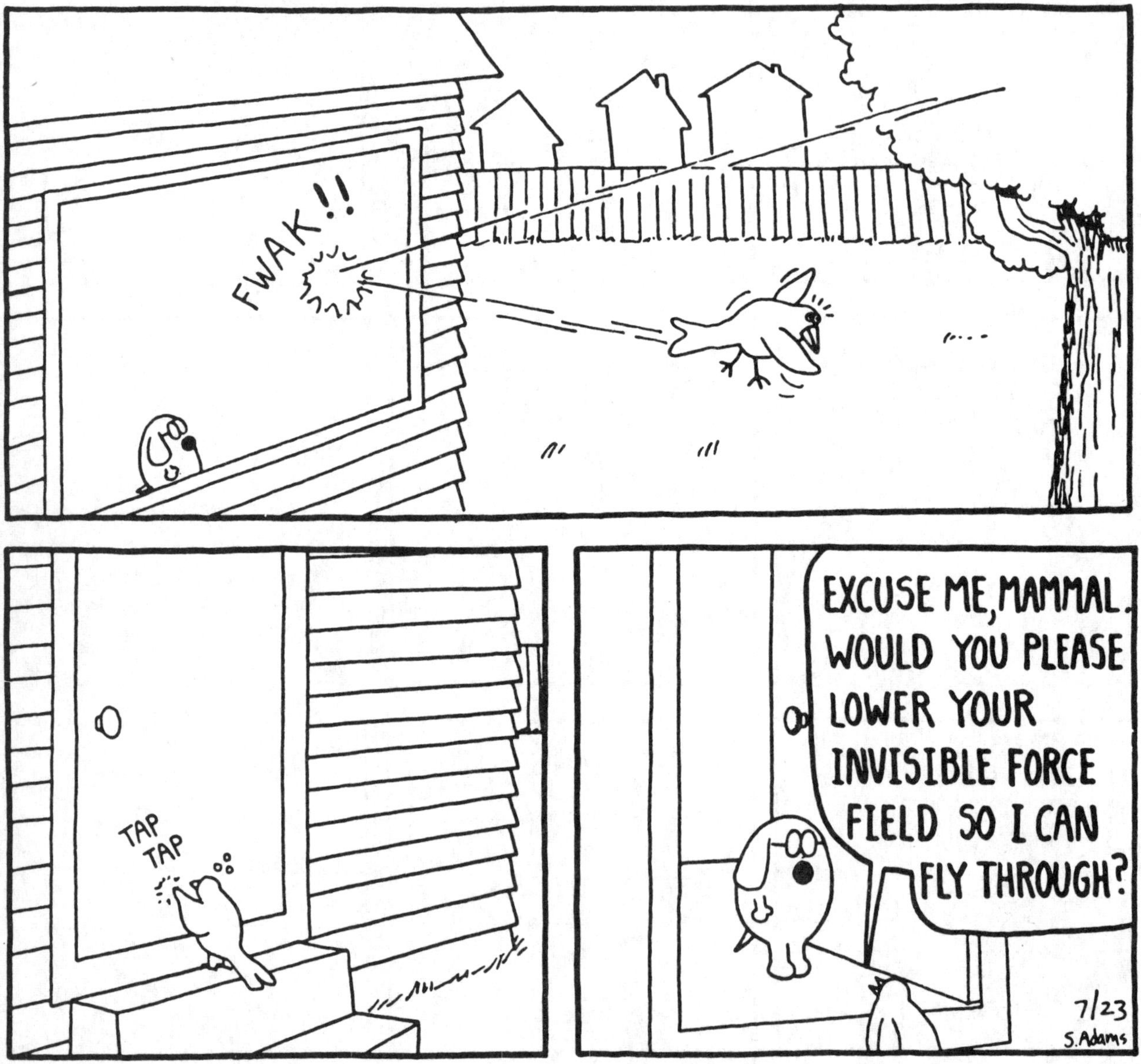
FWAK!!
TAP TAP
EXCUSE ME, MAMMAL. WOULD YOU PLEASE LOWER YOUR INVISIBLE FORCE FIELD SO I CAN FLY THROUGH?
7/23
S. Adams

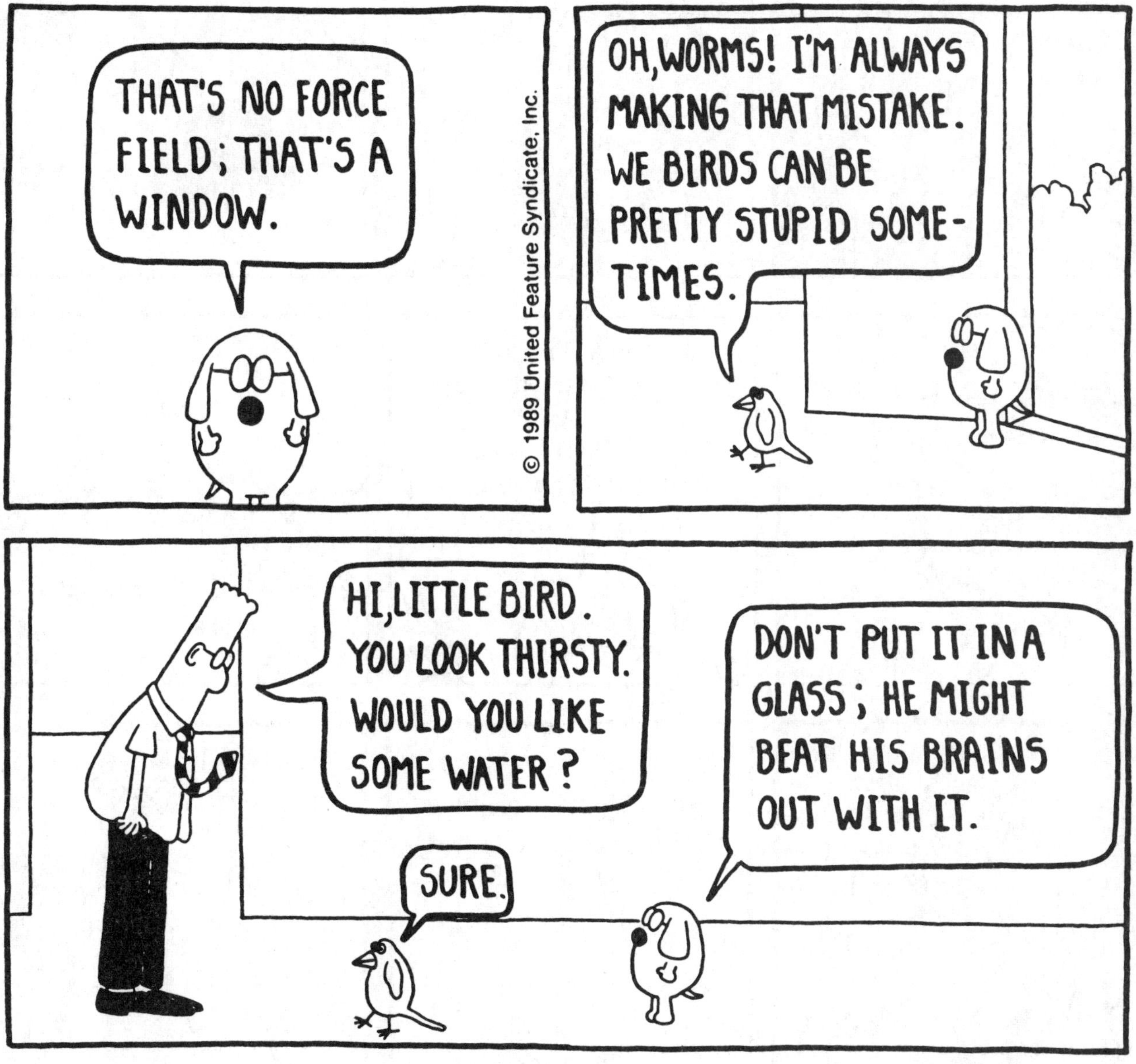
THAT'S NO FORCE FIELD; THAT'S A WINDOW.
© 1989 United Feature Syndicate, Inc.
OH, WORMS! I'M ALWAYS MAKING THAT MISTAKE. WE BIRDS CAN BE PRETTY STUPID SOME-TIMES.
HI, LITTLE BIRD. YOU LOOK THIRSTY. WOULD YOU LIKE SOME WATER?
SURE.
DON'T PUT IT IN A GLASS; HE MIGHT BEAT HIS BRAINS OUT WITH IT.

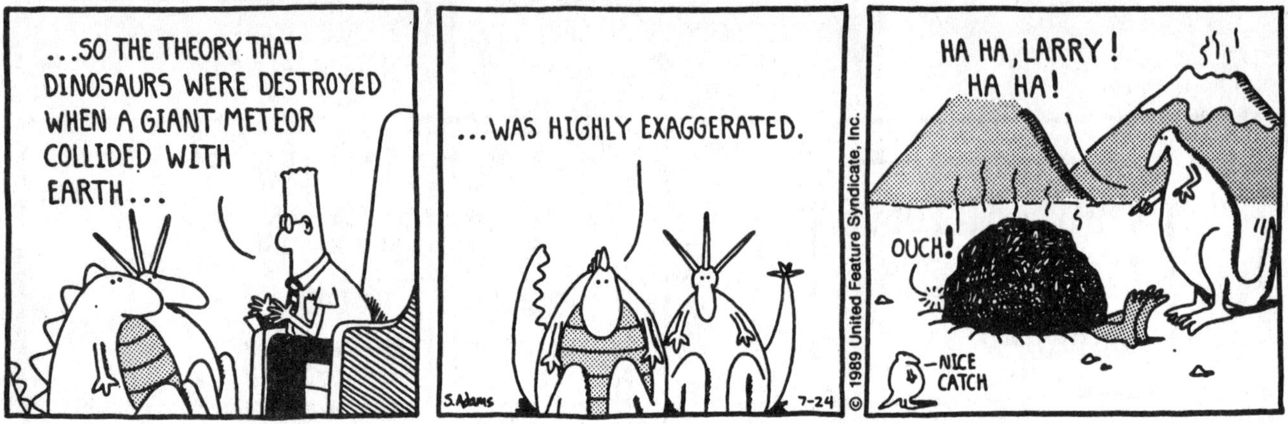
...SO THE THEORY THAT DINOSAURS WERE DESTROYED WHEN A GIANT METEOR COLLIDED WITH EARTH...
...WAS HIGHLY EXAGGERATED.
S. Adams 7-24
HA HA, LARRY! HA HA!
OUCH!
NICE CATCH

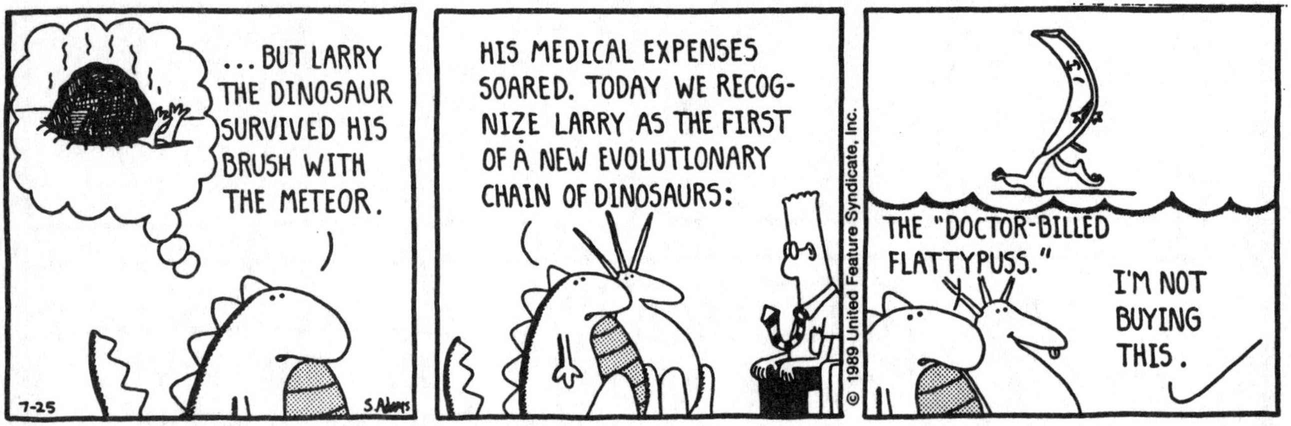
...BUT LARRY THE DINOSAUR SURVIVED HIS BRUSH WITH THE METEOR.
7-25 S. Adams
HIS MEDICAL EXPENSES SOARED. TODAY WE RECOGNIZE LARRY AS THE FIRST OF A NEW EVOLUTIONARY CHAIN OF DINOSAURS:
THE "DOCTOR-BILLED FLATTYPUSS."
I'M NOT BUYING THIS.

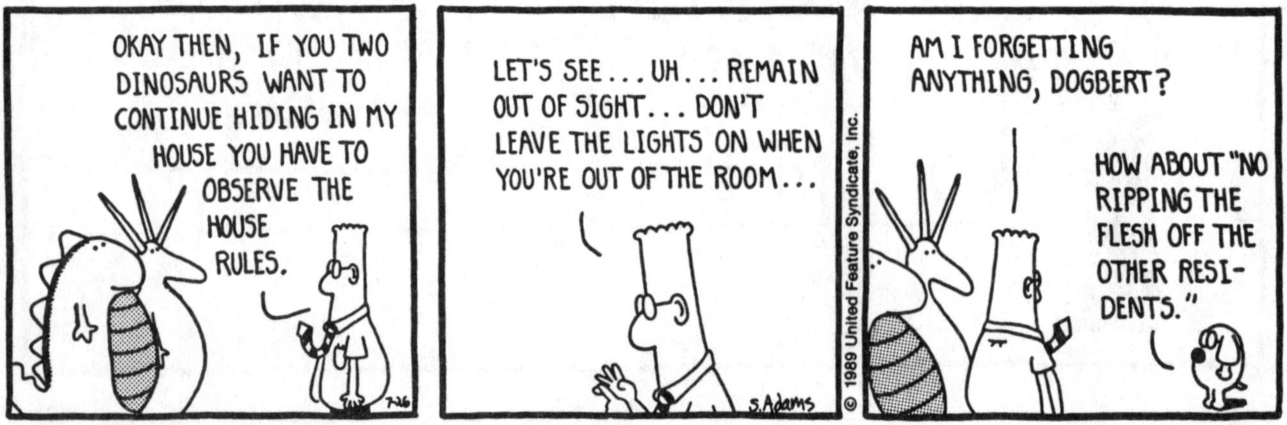
OKAY THEN, IF YOU TWO DINOSAURS WANT TO CONTINUE HIDING IN MY HOUSE YOU HAVE TO OBSERVE THE HOUSE RULES.
7-26
LET'S SEE... UH... REMAIN OUT OF SIGHT... DON'T LEAVE THE LIGHTS ON WHEN YOU'RE OUT OF THE ROOM...
S. Adams
AM I FORGETTING ANYTHING, DOGBERT?
HOW ABOUT "NO RIPPING THE FLESH OFF THE OTHER RESIDENTS."

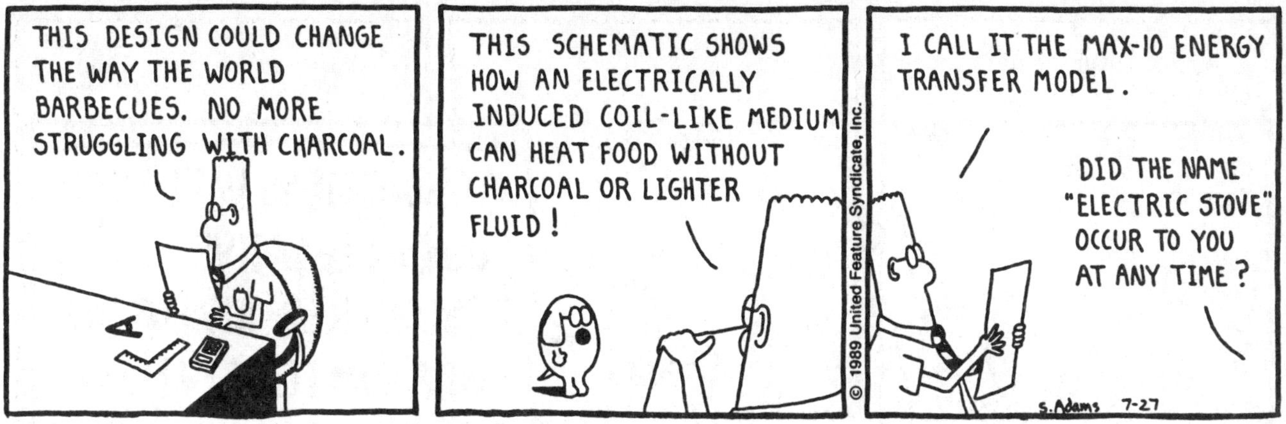
THIS DESIGN COULD CHANGE THE WAY THE WORLD BARBECUES. NO MORE STRUGGLING WITH CHARCOAL.
THIS SCHEMATIC SHOWS HOW AN ELECTRICALLY INDUCED COIL-LIKE MEDIUM CAN HEAT FOOD WITHOUT CHARCOAL OR LIGHTER FLUID!
© 1989 United Feature Syndicate, Inc.
I CALL IT THE MAX-10 ENERGY TRANSFER MODEL.
DID THE NAME "ELECTRIC STOVE" OCCUR TO YOU AT ANY TIME?
S.Adams 7-27

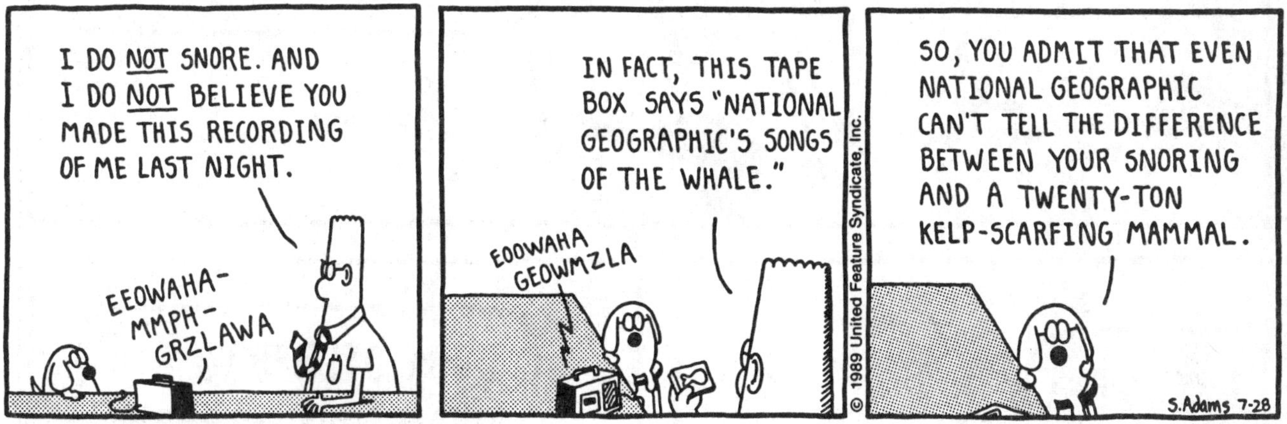
I DO NOT SNORE. AND I DO NOT BELIEVE YOU MADE THIS RECORDING OF ME LAST NIGHT.
EEOWAHA-MMPH-GRZLAWA
IN FACT, THIS TAPE BOX SAYS "NATIONAL GEOGRAPHIC'S SONGS OF THE WHALE."
EOOWAHA GEOWMZLA
© 1989 United Feature Syndicate, Inc.
SO, YOU ADMIT THAT EVEN NATIONAL GEOGRAPHIC CAN'T TELL THE DIFFERENCE BETWEEN YOUR SNORING AND A TWENTY-TON KELP-SCARFING MAMMAL.
S.Adams 7-28

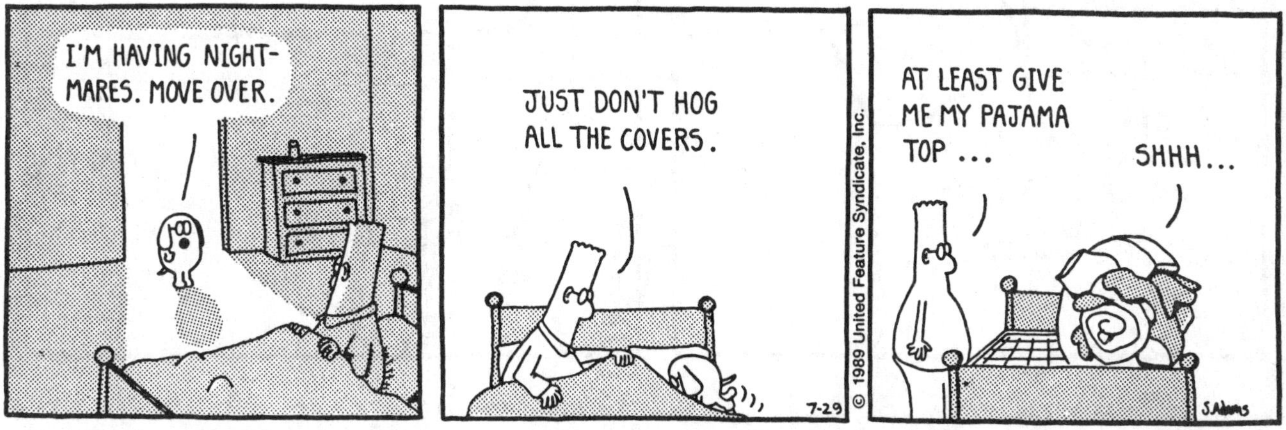
I'M HAVING NIGHT-MARES. MOVE OVER.
JUST DON'T HOG ALL THE COVERS.
7-29
© 1989 United Feature Syndicate, Inc.
AT LEAST GIVE ME MY PAJAMA TOP ...
SHHH...
S.Adams

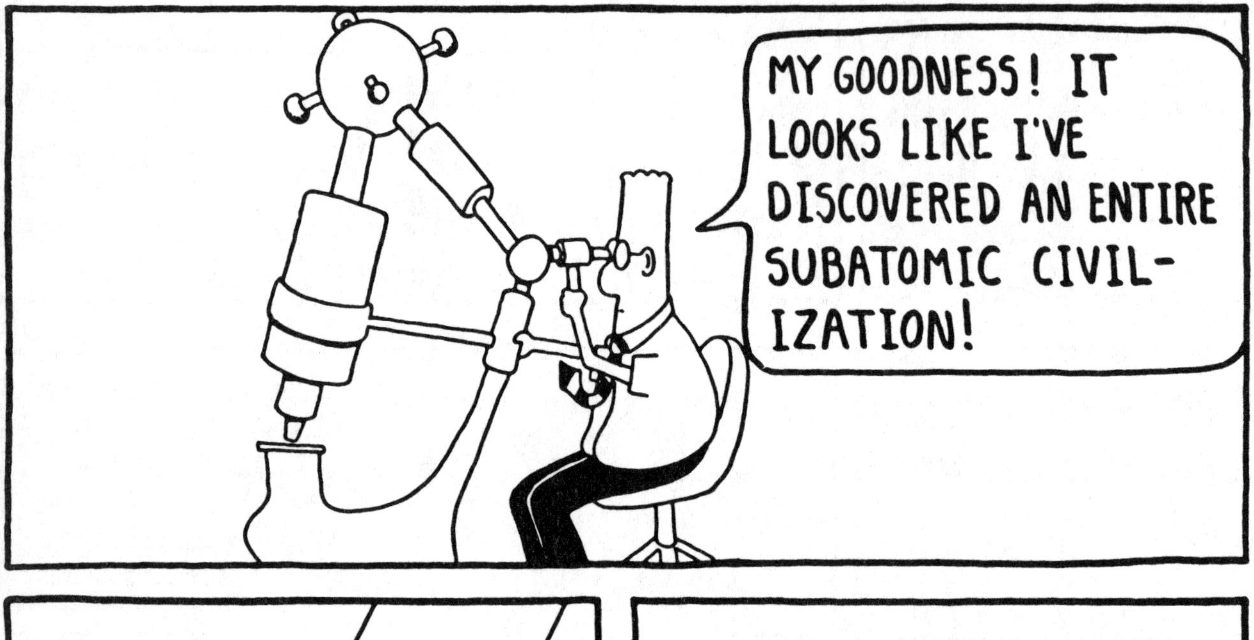
MY GOODNESS! IT LOOKS LIKE I'VE DISCOVERED AN ENTIRE SUBATOMIC CIVIL- IZATION!
HEY! WHAT ARE YOU STARING AT ?!!
I AM DILBERT. I MEAN YOU NO HARM.

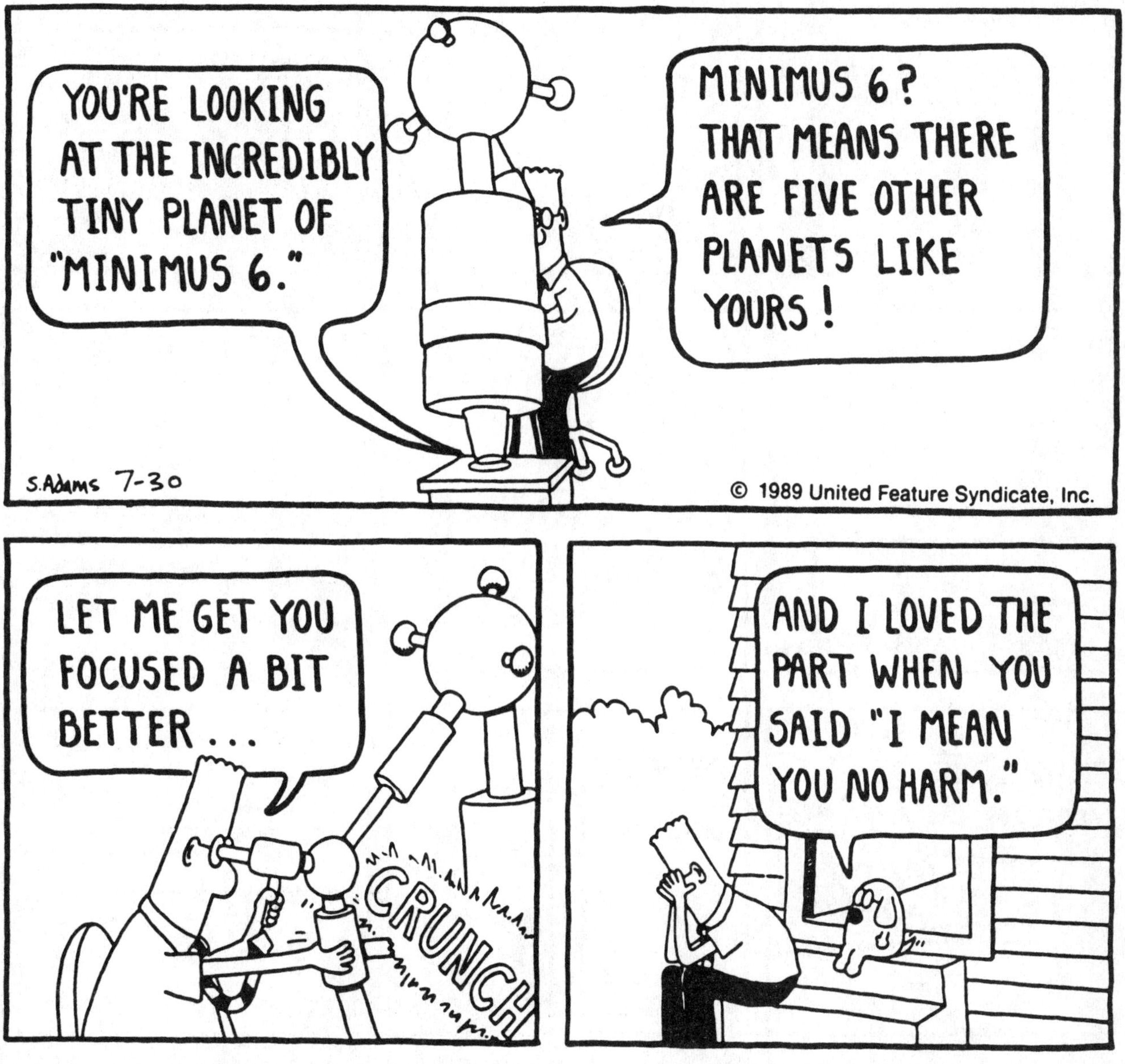
YOU'RE LOOKING AT THE INCREDIBLY TINY PLANET OF "MINIMUS 6."
MINIMUS 6? THAT MEANS THERE ARE FIVE OTHER PLANETS LIKE YOURS!
S.Adams 7-30
© 1989 United Feature Syndicate, Inc.
LET ME GET YOU FOCUSED A BIT BETTER . . .
CRUNCH
AND I LOVED THE PART WHEN YOU SAID "I MEAN YOU NO HARM."

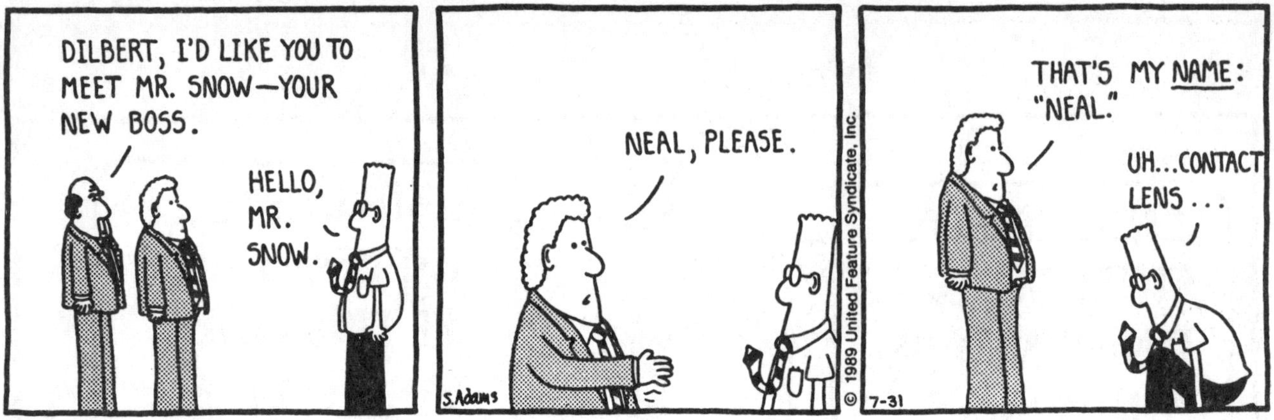
DILBERT, I'D LIKE YOU TO MEET MR. SNOW—YOUR NEW BOSS.
HELLO, MR. SNOW.
NEAL, PLEASE.
S.Adams
© 1989 United Feature Syndicate, Inc.
THAT'S MY NAME: "NEAL."
UH...CONTACT LENS...
7-31

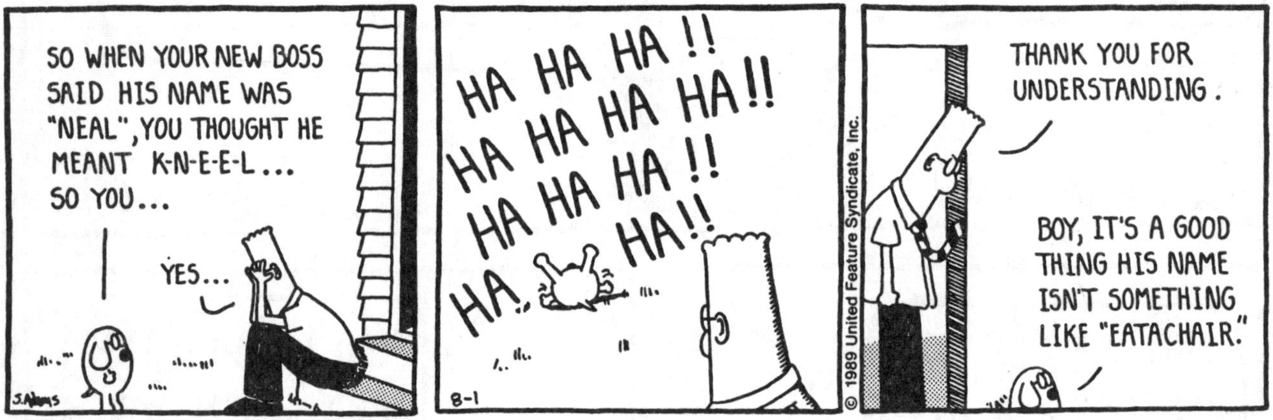
SO WHEN YOUR NEW BOSS SAID HIS NAME WAS "NEAL", YOU THOUGHT HE MEANT K-N-E-E-L... SO YOU...
YES...
S.Adams
HA HA HA!! HA HA HA HA!! HA HA HA!! HA HA!!
8-1
© 1989 United Feature Syndicate, Inc.
THANK YOU FOR UNDERSTANDING.
BOY, IT'S A GOOD THING HIS NAME ISN'T SOMETHING LIKE "EATACHAIR."

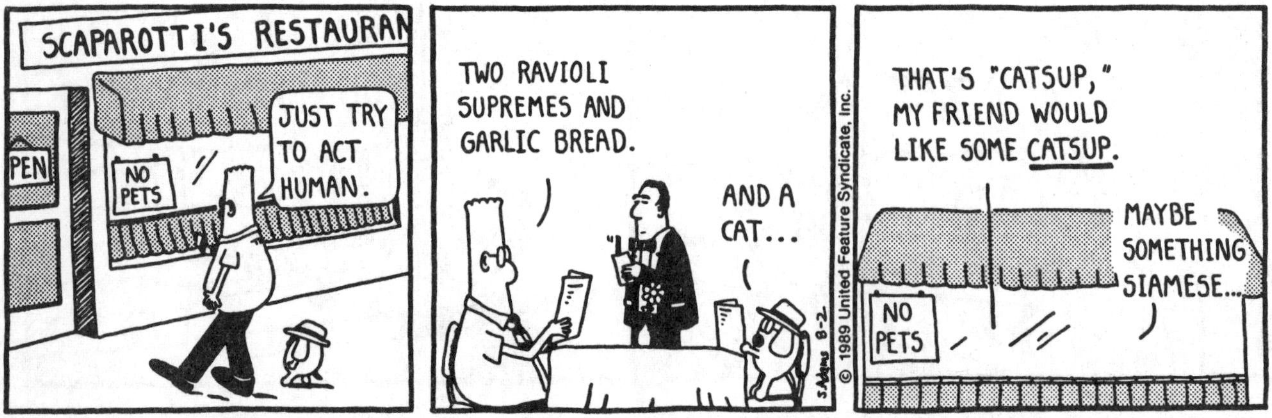
SCAPAROTTI'S RESTAURAN
PEN
NO PETS
JUST TRY TO ACT HUMAN.
TWO RAVIOLI SUPREMES AND GARLIC BREAD.
AND A CAT...
S.Adams 8-2
© 1989 United Feature Syndicate, Inc.
THAT'S "CATSUP," MY FRIEND WOULD LIKE SOME CATSUP.
MAYBE SOMETHING SIAMESE...
NO PETS

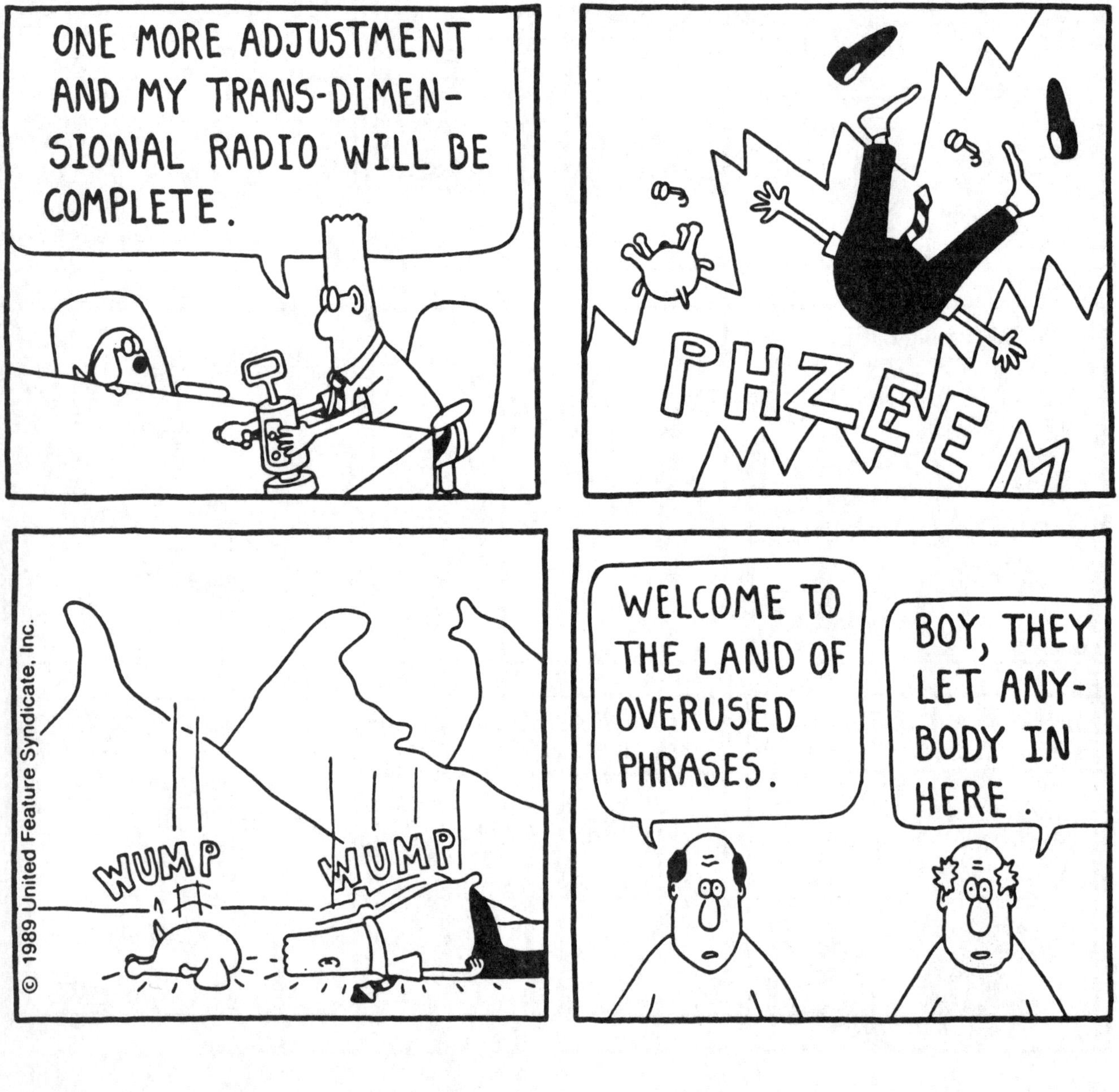
ONE MORE ADJUSTMENT AND MY TRANS-DIMENSIONAL RADIO WILL BE COMPLETE.
PHZEEEM
© 1989 United Feature Syndicate, Inc.
WUMP
WUMP
WELCOME TO THE LAND OF OVERUSED PHRASES.
BOY, THEY LET ANYBODY IN HERE.

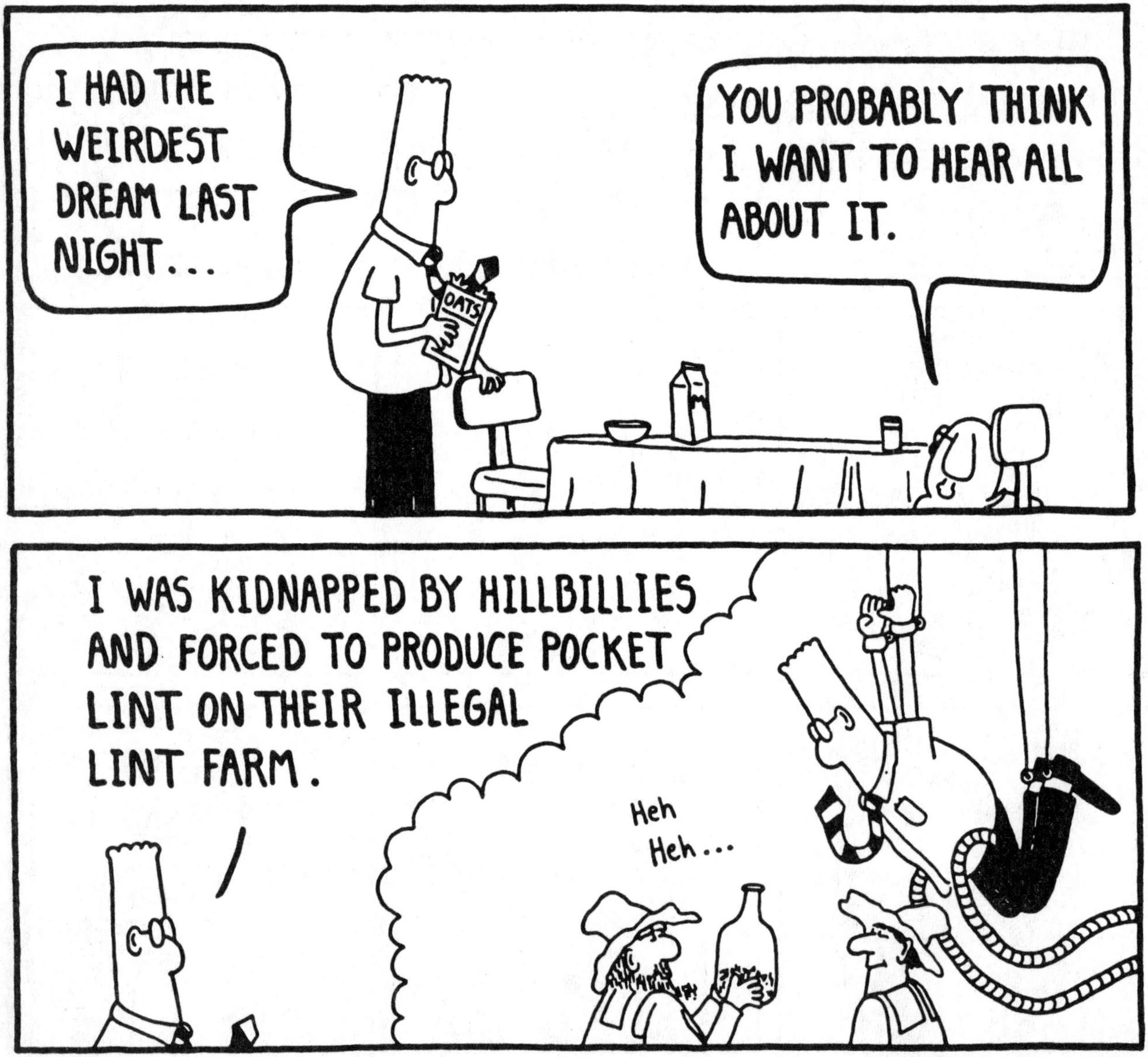
I HAD THE WEIRDEST DREAM LAST NIGHT...
YOU PROBABLY THINK I WANT TO HEAR ALL ABOUT IT.
OATS
I WAS KIDNAPPED BY HILLBILLIES AND FORCED TO PRODUCE POCKET LINT ON THEIR ILLEGAL LINT FARM.
Heh Heh...

...OR DOGASTROPHIC.
SOON THE FIELD STABILIZES, AND THE THREAT IS FORGOTTEN.
THAT REMINDS ME — WHAT'S FOR SUPPER TONIGHT?
9/3
S.Adams

ALWAYS POSTPONE MEETINGS WITH TIME-WASTING MORONS

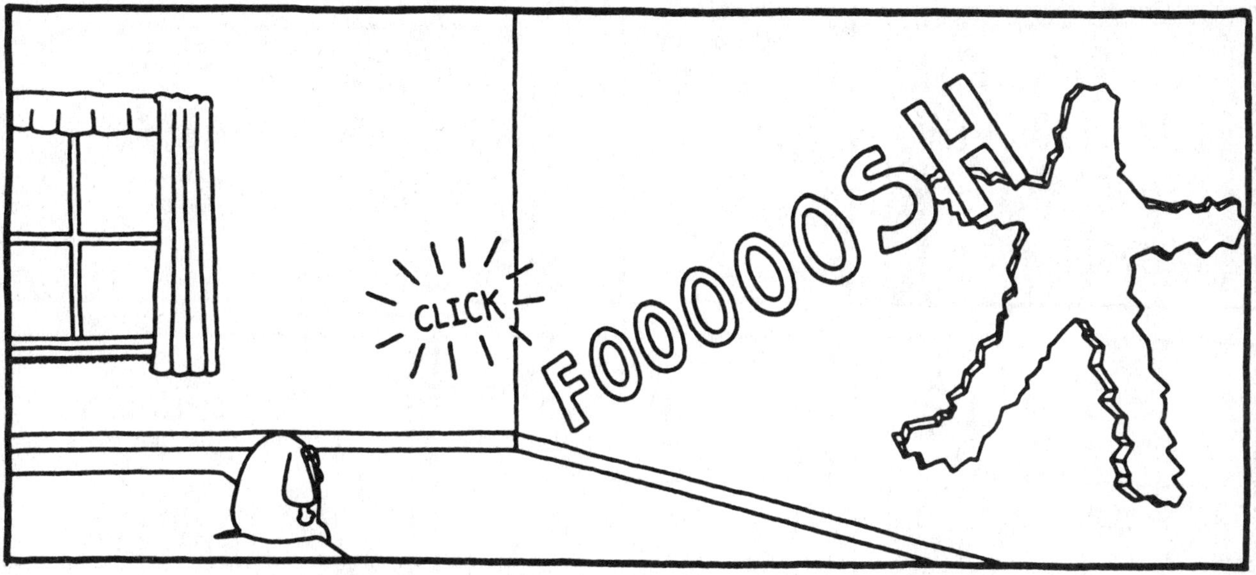
CLICK
FOOOOOOSH

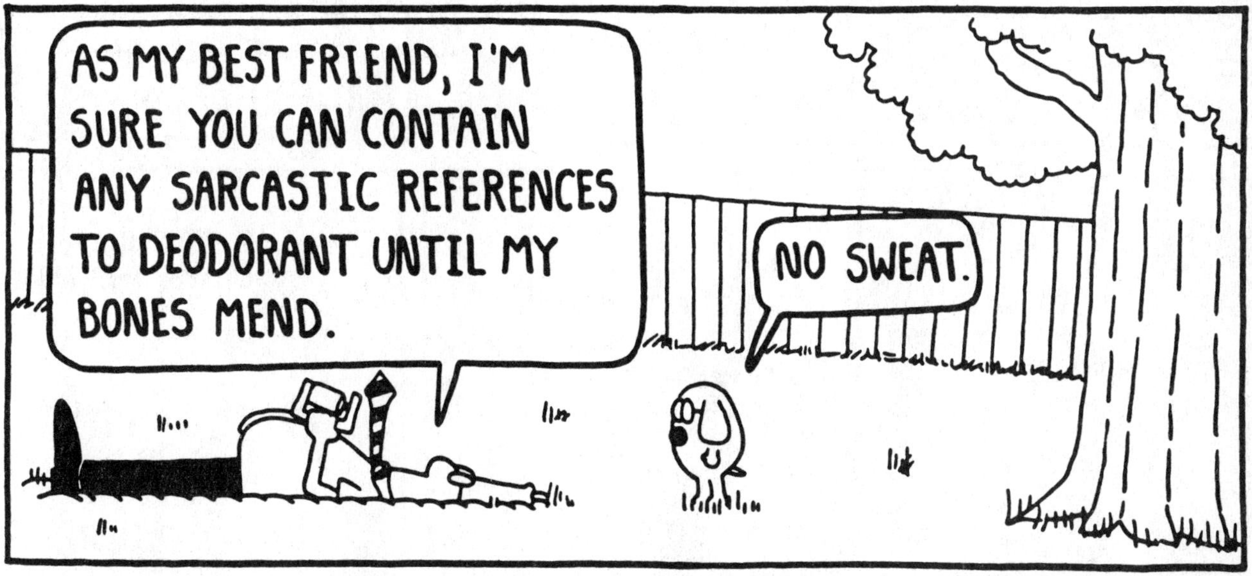
AS MY BEST FRIEND, I'M SURE YOU CAN CONTAIN ANY SARCASTIC REFERENCES TO DEODORANT UNTIL MY BONES MEND.
NO SWEAT.

ALWAYS POSTPONE MEETINGS WITH TIME-WASTING MORONS

10-8 © 1989 United Feature Syndicate, Inc. S.Adams

ALWAYS POSTPONE MEETINGS WITH TIME-WASTING MORONS

ALWAYS POSTPONE MEETINGS WITH TIME-WASTING MORONS

Other *Dilbert* titles published by Boxtree:

Shave The Whales